Jutting from the floor of the Smoky Hill River Valley, between Oakley and Scott City, are the Monument Rocks. These rocks are all that remain of the shale and chalk beds that at one time completely filled the Smoky Hill River Valley.

GEOGRAPHY
OF KANSAS

HUBER SELF
Assistant Professor of Geography
Kansas State University
Manhattan

HARLOW PUBLISHING CORPORATION
Oklahoma City—Chattanooga

Harlow State Geography Series

John W. Morris, Consulting Editor

Browne—*Missouri Geography*

Buchanan—*Louisiana Geography*

Law—*Tennessee Geography*

Lemert and Harrelson— *North Carolina Geography*

Morris—*Oklahoma Geography*

Schwendeman—*Geography of Kentucky*

Scott—*Texas Geography*

Self—*Geography of Kansas*

Bell—*Geography of Georgia*

DEDICATION

To the boys and girls of Kansas, who will help to make our State a greater Kansas, this book is dedicated.

PREFACE

Each person needs to understand the surroundings in which he lives. He needs to know the geographic conditions of his state. An earnest effort has been made in this book to present the principal facts of Kansas geography in a form simple and attractive enough to interest boys and girls in the upper grades and junior high school. The material is presented with enough detail and interpretation to make the book of value to older students as well.

The various topics discussed are handled on a state-wide basis. The young student will have a better understanding by studying all of a particular subject at one time. The presentation of the whole topic to the student enables him to understand the causes and the effects, the whys and wherefores of the problem under discussion. For example, if the student understands the distribution of climate and landforms for the state as a whole, he is more able to explain land use and population locations for the entire state. Maps, tables, pictures, and graphs are used to help tie all materials together to make a complete picture.

The names used for the various physical, agricultural, and other regions are those commonly used in the publications of the Kansas Academy of Science, Kansas State Board of Agriculture, Kansas Industrial Development Commission, the State Geological Survey of Kansas, and more advanced publications.

CONTENTS

TABLES

MAPS

COLORED PLATES

Chapter 1

AN INTRODUCTION TO KANSAS

Kansas is one of the great states of the United States. Since January 29, 1861, when it was admitted as the thirty-fourth state in the Union, Kansas has contributed much to the growth and development of the country. The people of the state have been and are national leaders. Several nationally known persons—President Dwight D. Eisenhower, editor and author William Allen White, Vice-President Charles Curtis, and Senator Arthur Capper— have claimed Kansas as their home. Good soil, a healthful climate, and many different kinds of minerals have aided the people in developing the state and making it great.

Geography contributes more useful knowledge about an area than any other subject. The geography of Kansas is all about us. Rivers, lakes, hills, valleys, plains, sunshine, wind, rain, native grasses and trees, as well as other things made by nature, make up the natural or physical surroundings. Roads, man-made lakes, fields of wheat and corn, coal mines, airfields, highways, towns, cities, and all things made or caused by man form the cultural surroundings. The number and kind of people in a place are also a part of our surroundings. *Geography* is a study of the ways in which people are influenced by their surroundings and

Kansas Industrial Development Commission

The Eisenhower Home. The boyhood home of President Dwight D. Eisenhower is located in Abilene. The building at the right is the Eisenhower Museum.

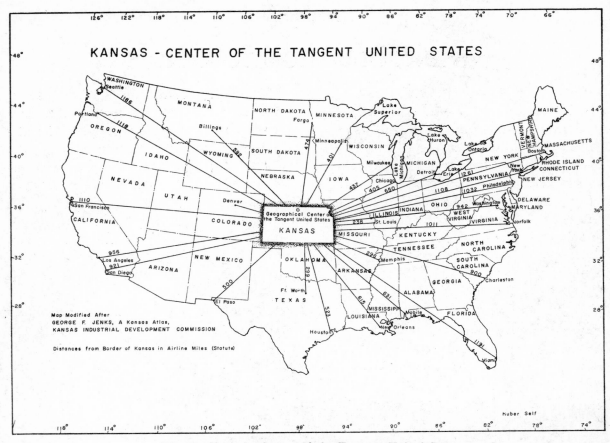

Map 1. Kansas—Center of the Tangent United States

how they, in turn, influence and change these same surroundings. Geography is also a study of the distribution of both nature and man's activities. We, then, are a part of geography, for we change and influence our surroundings, and our surroundings change and influence us.

The people in Kansas, like people in all other parts of the world, must work with nature to produce food, clothing, and shelter. Where people and nature work together, both are productive, for they are making the cultural surroundings which help both. Where people and nature do not work together, both suffer and neither is productive. The first part of our study of the geography of Kansas will be to find out where

Kansas is located and what its physical surroundings are. Next we shall study about the people of Kansas. Lastly, we shall study the cultural surroundings these people have made for themselves.

We wish to know Kansas well so that we can understand the problems that arise, and be able, as good citizens, to do our part in making the state productive and beautiful. Knowledge of the progress and development within the state at present, and an idea of its resources and possibilities, bring a greater pride and appreciation for our homeland. The more we know about Kansas, and the more we do for Kansas, the prouder we can be of our home state.

Location and Boundaries

Location is one of the most important facts about a place or an area. Kansas is fortunate in this respect, for Kansas is the heart of the forty-eight continuous states. Its central position within the nation is shown by the distances from its borders to the boundaries of the United States (Map 1). From the eastern boundary of Kansas to the Atlantic Coast is 1,100 miles; from the western boundary of the state it is 1,130 miles to the Pacific Ocean; from the Kansas-Nebraska border to Canada is a distance of approximately 620 miles, and from the southern border of Kansas to Mexico it is about 700 miles. Although Kansas, as a state, is not in the exact center of the United States, the center of the nation, not including Alaska and Hawaii, is in Kansas. The geographical center of the United States is located in Smith County about four miles north and eleven miles east of Smith Center, or one mile north and one mile west of Lebanon.

The global location of Kansas is from 37° to 40° north latitude and from approximately 94° 37′ to 102° 03′ west longitude. The *latitude* should be thought of as indicating distance north of the Equator, and the *longitude* indicates distance west from the Prime Meridian. The latitudes of Kansas are about two-fifths the distance from the Equator to the North Pole.

Although Kansas is one of the larger states of the nation, it is bordered by only four other states. Along its southern edge, Kansas has a common boundary with Oklahoma for over 411 miles. The northern boundary, which is almost 357 miles long, borders Nebraska. Along its western side Kansas borders Colorado for more than 207 miles. Only along the eastern border of the state is the Kansas boundary not a straight line. Here the broad, winding Missouri River separates Kansas and Missouri as it winds back and forth across the plains. From the mouth of the Kansas River the boundary extends straight south to the Oklahoma border, a distance of almost 143 miles (Map 1).

Area

Kansas, since it ranks fourteenth in size, is one of the larger states of the United States. Its area of 82,276 square miles makes Kansas larger than any state east of the Mississippi River. When compared in area with some of the western states, however, the size of Kansas does not seem so great.

Kansas Industrial Development Commission

Marker showing the geographic center of the forty-eight adjoining states of the United States. It is located two miles northwest of Lebanon and is visited by thousands of persons each year.

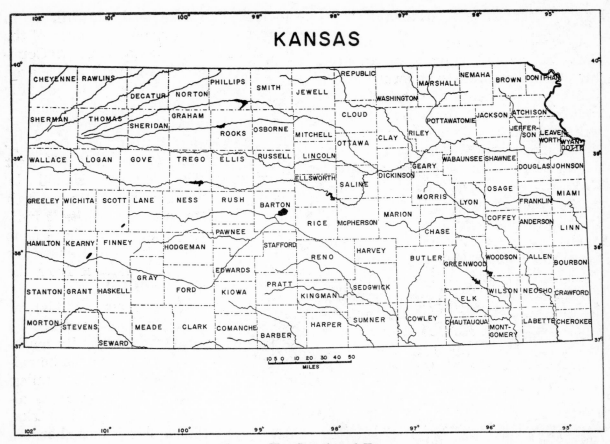

Map 2. The Counties of Kansas

Nevertheless, Kansas is larger than each of the states which border it, except Colorado.

Texas, the largest state in the continuous area of the United States, has an area of 267,339 square miles; that makes it a little more than three times as large as Kansas (Map 1). Alaska, however, has an area of 586,400 square miles and is a little more than seven times larger than Kansas. Kansas is more than sixty-eight times greater in area than Rhode Island, the smallest of the states. In fact, Kansas has a larger area than all six of the New England states—Maine, New Hampshire, Vermont, Massachusetts, Rhode Island, and Connecticut—combined.

Kansas is larger than several of the leading nations of the world. None of the Central American countries has as great an area as Kansas. The important country of Korea, in Asia, has about the same area. Kansas is much larger than Belgium, Netherlands, Austria, or Greece. Even the important country of England is only about two-thirds the size of Kansas.

Kansas is divided into 105 counties. The largest of these is Butler, which has an area of 1,445 square miles. This county alone is larger than the state of Rhode Island. Fifteen counties have areas greater than 1,000 square miles. The smallest of the 105 counties is Wyandotte. It has an area of only 151 square miles (Map 2).

Not all the surface of Kansas is land.

4

The lakes and ponds that have been built cover almost 250 square miles. As more of these lakes are formed, the amount of land surface will decrease. The largest bodies of water are man-made lakes where dams have been built across rivers.

Symbols of Kansas

The state seal of Kansas is an important symbol of the state. The seal illustrates the importance of agriculture and commerce to the state by showing a man plowing and a steamboat on a river. It also shows the pioneer spirit, for in the background is a train of ox-drawn wagons moving west. Across the top is the motto "Ad astra per aspera" which means "To the stars through difficulty." The state seal forms the center of the blue flag of Kansas. The flag also has on it a sunflower which is placed above the seal.

Other symbols of Kansas are the sunflower as the state flower; the meadow lark as the state bird; the cottonwood as the state tree; and the buffalo as the state animal. Kansas is often called the "Jayhawker State." The jayhawk is an imaginary bird. The name was first used by a group of raiders during the Civil War. One of the most famous songs of the United States is "Home on the Range." This song was written by Dr. Brewster Higley when he lived near Smith Center. He called the song "My Western Home." The title was changed after it was set to music. It is now the official song of Kansas.

Kansas Geographical Names

Kansas was named for the Kansas River. The river, however, had received its name from the principal tribe of Indians living along it when first

Chamber of Commerce, Topeka

The State Capitol. The State Capitol in Topeka is one of our most important state symbols.

visited by white men. Like many Indian names, Kansas has been spelled in many different ways. For a long time the word was spelled Kanzas. Some of the other spellings have been Cansaz, Konzas, Canzon, and Kasas. Locally the Kansas River is better known as the Kaw River.

In addition to the Indian name of the state several cities, such as Medicine Lodge, Council Grove, Wichita, and Topeka, show the influence of Indians or Indian activity. A number of the counties were named after Indian tribes.

Many important place names are those of pioneers. For example, Marysville, in Marshall County, was named for the wife of Francis J. Marshall, who operated a ferry across Blue River where Marysville now stands. The county was named for Marshall. James A. Coffey, another pioneer, gave his name to Coffeyville. Fort Riley was named for General Bennett Riley who was stationed for some time in Kansas. Riley County was also named for the general. The city of Iola carries the name of the wife of J. C. Colborn, an early pioneer. Wilson County was named for Hiero T. Wilson, a pioneer trader who settled at Fort Scott. Many counties were named after soldiers and several for presidents or cabinet members. Clara Barton, the founder of the Red Cross, is the only woman to be honored by having a county named for her.

STUDENT ACTIVITIES

1. Study a large wall map of the United States. Locate Kansas and the states that border it.

2. Find Chicago, New Orleans, San Francisco, Seattle, Washington, New York, Houston, and other large American cities. Which direction is each from your home community?

3. Draw a map of Kansas and show where the states that border it are located.

4. Get a road map of Kansas either from your filling station operator or by writing the Kansas Highway Commission, Topeka, Kansas. Locate your home community, county seat, and neighboring towns.

5. Find the scale of miles on your Kansas map. How far is it from your home to Topeka, Wichita, Dodge City, Kansas City, Liberal, Scott City, and Baxter Springs?

6. Look up the areas of several other states. How many of these are less than half as big as Kansas? What states are more than twice as large as Kansas?

7. List several reasons why you are proud of Kansas.

8. What can you do to make Kansas a better state in which to live?

9. Why are you a part of the geography of Kansas?

10. What latitude lines form a part of the boundary of Kansas? With what state or states do they form the boundary?

11. What is the greatest east to west distance across Kansas? North to south?

12. What counties are named after important Kansas leaders?

13. Why is the location of a Kansas a fortunate one?

14. What countries have a smaller area than the state of Kansas?

15. Make a list of the physical surroundings you can see from your classroom window. Make a list of the cultural surroundings that you can see.

6

Chapter 2

THE LAND OF KANSAS

Kansas is a plains state. It differs greatly from the neighboring state of Colorado in that it has no high mountains. Neither is there a large plateau area like the one located in southern Missouri, although a part of that plateau does extend into the southeastern corner of the state. Nevertheless, Kansas is an attractive state with a variety of rolling plains and hill lands. The surface features of the eastern part of the state differ greatly from those in the western part. Kansas also differs from some of its neighboring states in that it has no large forest areas. However, many trees grow along the streams, in the hill sections, and many other places where they have been planted. The chief natural vegetation of the state is the rich grass upon which large numbers of cattle feed. The land of Kansas offers many beautiful places to build cities and towns or to develop farms and ranches.

Elevations

Kansas is about 510 miles northwest of the Gulf of Mexico, and it is to the Gulf of Mexico that all the water flows which runs off the surface of Kansas. This means that Kansas is higher than the land to the east and south of it

Kansas Industrial Development Commission

A Typical Plains Farm. Much of Kansas is level plains. In such areas there are many large wheat farms and ranches.

7

State Geological Survey of Kansas

The High Plains near Hill City. The High Plains are noted for their vast areas of level land and wheat. This scene, taken south of Hill City in Graham County, shows how far one can see in such a landscape.

through which this water drains. The number of feet that the surface of Kansas is higher than the Gulf of Mexico is called its *elevation* above sea level. Where the Verdigris River leaves Kansas, in the southeastern part of Montgomery County, the elevation is 686 feet. This is the lowest point in the state. From this low level the land rises higher and higher until it reaches its highest point in the state along the western boundary. This highest point of elevation, 4,135 feet, is in the southwestern corner of Wallace County.

One way to show the change of elevation in Kansas from the valley of the Verdigris River to the highest point is on a physical map. This is a map in colors and lines—the lines are called contour lines. A *contour line* is a line that connects places and points having the same elevation. Certain elevations above sea level are selected, such as 1,000 feet, and the contour line is drawn to connect all points at this elevation. All points lower than 1,000 feet will, then, be colored green. The next contour line can then be drawn at 2,000 feet, and all the land above the 1,000 foot contour line, but lower than 2,000 feet, will be colored yellow. This continues until you can see by the map where the different elevations above sea level are, and how much each area is. Such a map is very useful in studying weather, climate, and stream flow. Of course, such a map may have contour lines at elevation intervals of 500 or even 100 feet or less without coloring the land between them. This is often done on maps of a smaller area and the maps are called *topographic maps*.

Topographic maps have been made for much of the land area of North America. For convenience, The United States Coast and Geodetic Survey placed a marker in North America

8

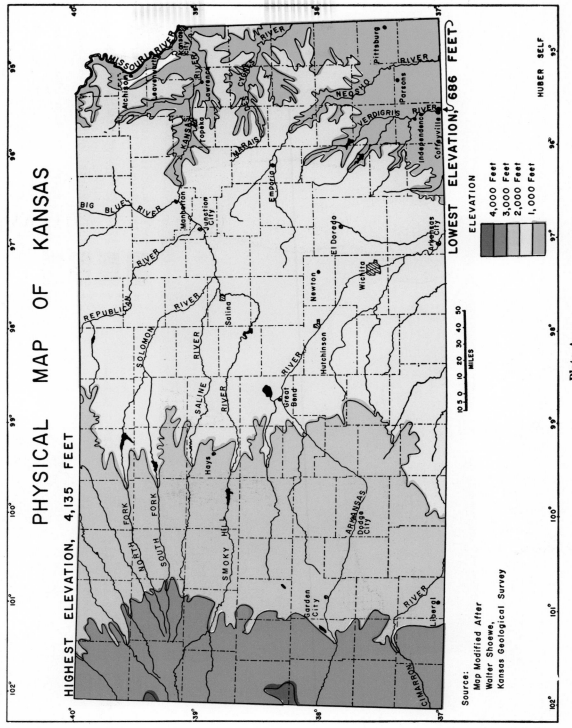

PHYSICAL MAP OF KANSAS

HIGHEST ELEVATION, 4,135 FEET

LOWEST ELEVATION, 686 FEET

HUBER SELF

ELEVATION

4,000 Feet
3,000 Feet
2,000 Feet
1,000 Feet

MILES

Source:
Map Modified After
Walter Shoewe,
Kansas Geological Survey

Plate A

NATURAL VEGETATION MAP OF KANSAS

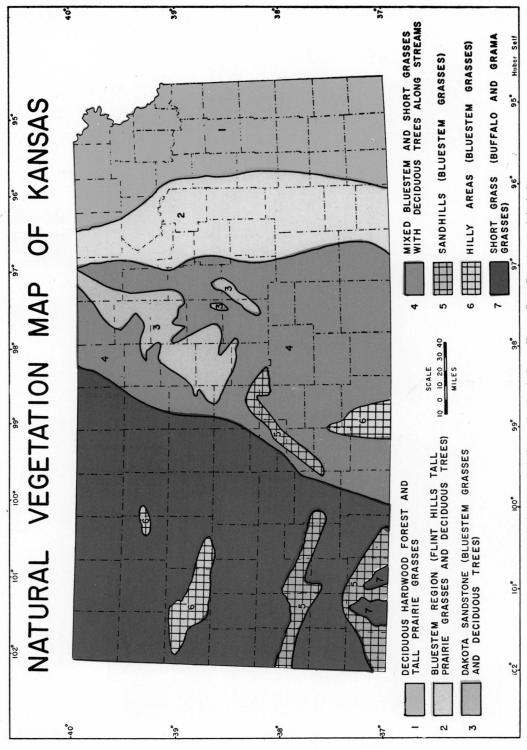

1   DECIDUOUS HARDWOOD FOREST AND TALL PRAIRIE GRASSES

2   BLUESTEM REGION (FLINT HILLS TALL PRAIRIE GRASSES AND DECIDUOUS TREES)

3   DAKOTA SANDSTONE (BLUESTEM GRASSES AND DECIDUOUS TREES)

4   MIXED BLUESTEM AND SHORT GRASSES WITH DECIDUOUS TREES ALONG STREAMS

5   SANDHILLS (BLUESTEM GRASSES)

6   HILLY AREAS (BLUESTEM GRASSES)

7   SHORT GRASS (BUFFALO AND GRAMA GRASSES)

SCALE

10 0 10 20 30 40

MILES

Huber Self

Modified from *Grasses of Kansas*, by Frank Gates, Kansas State Department of Agriculture

Plate B

from which all federal mapping in the United States, Canada, and Mexico originates. This bronze marker was placed in a concrete slab. It is located in a pasture in Osborn County, Kansas, about forty miles south of the marker that indicates the geographic center of the forty-eight adjoining states. This marker is known as the Geodetic Datum of North America. Location of all places on maps of North America are shown to be a certain distance from this point. Scientifically the Geodetic Datum of North America is a more significant marker than is the better known geographic center marker.

A topographic map shows local relief. *Local relief* is the roughness or smoothness of the land at any given place. In the area between the 1,000- and 2,000-foot contour lines is much rough land. In Barton, Russell, Lin- coln, Mitchell, and other counties are many hills known as the Blue Hills and the Smoky Hills. All of this area has an elevation of more than 1,000 feet and a few places have elevations above 2,000 feet. The hills, however, have a local relief of usually fifty to 100 feet. Since these amounts are less than 1,000 feet, which is the difference between the contour lines, they do not show on the map. The local relief of any area may affect the ways in which the people of an area make a living. If the land is too rough and the hills too steep, the area cannot be used successfully for farming.

The Rocks of Kansas

Not all the land that is now Kansas was formed at the same time. *Geologists*, the people who study the rocks and the minerals of which the earth is

Rough Land in Sumner County. This area of rough land is located in Sumner County. The ledges are formed by a hard shale that does not erode as fast as the other materials.

Hilly Land in Doniphan County. This area of hilly country, located in Doniphan County, is typical of much of that part of Kansas formerly covered by glaciers. The hills were formed by the uneven deposition of material left by the glacier when it melted. The river is the Missouri.

composed, say that the formation of the land of Kansas required many millions of years. From their study of the different kinds of rocks, and the ways in which the rocks are put together, they tell us about the history of the earth long before man came to live upon it. From the geologists we learn that much of the area of present-day Kansas was covered by oceans and seas for long periods of time. During other periods of the past, some parts of Kansas stood high above the seas. When the land was above the level of the water, the winds and the rains eroded the rocks and wore them down.

A large part of western Kansas is covered with material—sand, gravel, silt, clay—that has been eroded from the Rocky Mountains. Water flowing eastward from the mountains carried this material and deposited it in the western part of the state forming a large area that is called the High Plains. Material has also been moved into northeastern Kansas by glaciers. During the great ice age of the earth one of these glaciers covered the area north of the Kansas River and east of the Big Blue River. A glacier, as it moves, pushes material ahead of it as well as carrying material in and on the ice. But when the ice of the glacier melts, it deposits the material it is carrying at that place. Thus, northeastern Kansas had a mixture of sand, rock, clay, gravel, and other material deposited on it that the glacier moved from the northern part of the United States and Canada. In most cases the

10

depositing of material by either water or ice was helpful for it made the soil richer, filled depressions, and, in some places made large areas suitable for farming.

The most common kinds of rocks in Kansas are shales, limestone, and sandstones. These three kinds of rocks are called *sedimentary rocks* for the particles which compose them. They are found at the surface in the eastern third of the state. The sandstone is made of grains of sand held together by such natural cements as iron, lime, and silica. The limestone is made up of fine particles of lime and from sea shells made of lime and silica. Shale is made from very fine-grained material called clay which comes from a variety of minerals. These rocks lie in layers and can be seen in many parts of the state where they project above the ground, or where broken fragments lie about on the surface. The best places to see these rock layers are in valleys where streams have cut through them. The importance of these rocks to us is that (1) they form the surface of the land on which we live and are a colorful and often spectacular part of our natural scenery; (2) our soils are derived from them; and (3) they are most useful as building material. Also, in some of these layers of rocks, and between them, we get such useful minerals as coal, gas, petroleum, lead, and zinc. Sedimentary rocks act as storage basins for ground water that can be obtained by drilling wells, or that may even flow out as springs.

These underlying sedimentary rocks of Kansas were formed in those shallow seas of long ago that covered what is now Kansas as well as a large part of the United States. If you look closely at limestone, you may find sea shells, now turned to stone, that are much like the sea shells you will find today. Also, in the sandstone you may find ripple marks such as are made in the sands

Department of Agronomy, Kansas State University

The Flint Hills in Riley County. The Flint Hills form an important region of Kansas. This picture, taken about 4.5 miles northwest of Manhattan in Riley County, shows the good pastures and the typical flint hills to be found throughout the region.

of the beach by the ocean waves. In these shallow seas billions of tiny organisms lived, many so small that it would be necessary to use a microscope to see them. As these organisms died they were buried in the muds. Layers of sedimentary rock covered them. Most geologists believe that after many ages had passed the organisms were changed to small particles of oil and gas. In some places enough of these oil and gas particles accumulated in the pores and crevices of the rock layers to form the present oil and gas fields of Kansas.

Into the shallow sea the rivers poured their flood waters and gradually covered its bottom with layers of sandstone, shale, and limestone in that order from the shore outward. As the sea was gradually filled, these rocks were in layers as they are today.

From time to time during the filling, the land was elevated. The sea water was drained away for a while and replaced by fresh water swamps. From the plant and animal life of these swamps came the coal we now use. The change from this swamp life to coal came about through the ages as the land sank again and other layers of sedimentary rock covered the swamps and their life, thus preserving the material. These processes of the sinking and rising of the land, the ebb and flow of the shallow sea, the laying down of sedimentary rocks, and the growth of swamp life were repeated many times so that today Kansas has many different layers of rocks with coal, oil, and gas either in them or between them. Finally, the land rose to stay above the level of the water and the seas drained away to return no more. Out of this

past, Kansas has gained a rich inheritance in rocks and minerals.

In addition to the sedimentary rocks, there are a few places in which igneous rocks are found in Kansas. *Igneous rocks* are formed from the hot, molten material that pushes up from the interior of the earth, is cooled, and becomes a solid. Granite is a good example of an igneous rock. Small areas of igneous rock can be seen in Woodson and Riley counties. They are of little value.

Surface Features

Kansas is a part of three great surface features of the western part of the United States. These are (1) the Great Plains in the western part of the state; (2) the Central Lowlands that cover most of the eastern part of Kansas; and (3) the Ozark Plateau in the southeastern corner of the state. These large divisions are too broad to be of much use locally in Kansas. Many of our local regions, such as the Flint Hills and the High Plains, have been left out.

The landscape of Kansas has much more variety than most people realize. As we look across our state we find three classes of surface features: (1) the plains which cover most of the western half of the state; (2) the hills and other rough lands such as those found in the Smoky Hills and Red Hills areas, or along the river bluffs of the Missouri River, and canyons; and (3) the bottom lands along the rivers. In many places the surface features attract much attention because of the shape of the rock formations or because of their color. People on vacation can see many interesting sights.

THE SURFACE FEATURES OF KANSAS

By RAYMOND C. MOORE

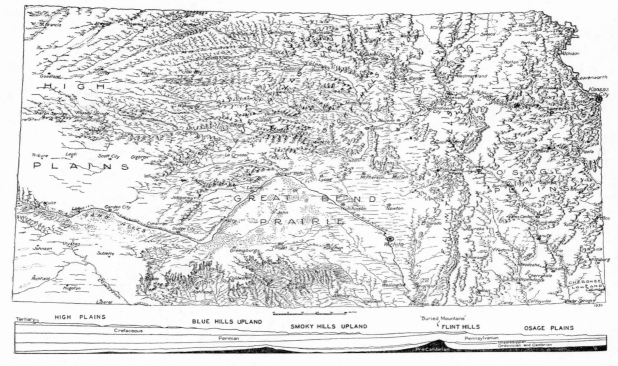

Map 3.   The Surface Features of Kansas

In many parts of Kansas, man has changed the surface. In Cherokee County great ridges of earth have been piled up where the surface has been scraped off so that coal could be mined. Some of these old pits have filled with water forming lakes. In other places the building of dams across rivers has also formed large lakes. In the drier parts of the state many wells have been dug and the water used for irrigation. The more you travel about Kansas, the greater the number of differences in the surface features you will see.

STUDENT ACTIVITIES

1. What does elevation mean? Where is the highest elevation in Kansas? Where is the lowest?

2. How are sedimentary rocks formed? What are three sedimentary rocks found in Kansas? Why are these rocks important?

3. What is a contour line? What is a topographic map? What location in Kansas is important in the making of topographic maps?

4. What does *local relief* mean? Describe the local relief of your community.

5. What is the work of a geologist? Why is this work important?

6. How are igneous rocks formed? Give an example of an igneous rock. Where are igneous rocks found in Kansas?

7. In parts of which three geographic regions of the United States is Kansas located? Look at a map of the United States and determine what other states are also partly in these regions.

13

8. What are the three large classes of surface features found in Kansas? In which part of the state could you find examples of each?

9. What proof is there that much of Kansas was once covered by the great prehistoric oceans?

10. Why is Kansas an attractive state? What are the most attractive and interesting landforms in your community?

11. Ask your teacher to show you a topographic map of the community in which you live. What is the elevation of your community?

12. In which part of the state are the roads the straightest? Why? In which part of the state do the roads curve the most? Why?

13. Study the county or area in which you live. What are the chief landforms? How are they used? In what ways has man changed these landforms?

14. Make a collection of rocks from various parts of Kansas. Classify these rocks. What are the most common kind of rocks in your community?

15. How do the physical features of your community influence the things the people do to make a living? In which part of the state do the physical features have the greatest influence? Why?

16. Define the following terms:
   sedimentary
   igneous
   metamorphic
   rock

17. Why is the study of geology important? Do any geologists live in your community? If so, why not invite them to talk with your group about the geology of your area?

Chapter 3

KANSAS WATERS

Water is one of the most important natural resources of Kansas. Long before the land that now forms the state was well known, people often thought of it as a very dry, or desert, country. In fact, most of the Great Plains, of which much of Kansas is a part, was called the Great American Desert. As explorers crossed and recrossed Kansas, they began to find many streams and rivers. Only a few lakes were found, however, and they were small. Kansas does not have nearly as much water as most eastern states and some parts of many of the western states. Since water is essential in agriculture, the development of manufacturing, and the growth of towns and cities, the people of Kansas have had to learn to use their water efficiently and wisely.

The water supply of Kansas comes from three sources—rivers, lakes, and ground water. The rivers differ greatly from one part of the state to the other. Most of the larger lakes have been formed by the building of dams across rivers, and most of the ground water is made available by drilling wells. In some places, however, the ground water comes to the surface in the form of springs.

Rivers

Rivers get their water in part from the rains that run off the surface, in part from springs, in part from the water of melting snow. A large amount of water soaks into the ground when the rainfall is slow and falling on level, sandy land. This water descends into the earth and may return to the surface in the form of a spring. Should the rainfall be hard, and the surface rocky and steep, most of the water will run off and find its way into small streams and creeks. The streams and creeks finally come together and form a river.

The rivers of Kansas differ greatly from place to place. In the western part of the state many rivers are broad, shallow, and often filled with sand. Some, however, like the Smoky Hill River are deep. In other parts of the state, where the rivers are flowing through hill country, they may be swift and fairly clear. The characteristics of a river are determined by the kind of rocks and the type of country over which it is flowing.

The two principal rivers of Kansas are the Arkansas and the Kansas (Plate A). All large rivers in the southern half of the state eventually flow into the Arkansas River. Most of the important rivers in the northern part of the state flow into the Kansas. The Marais des Cygnes is the only large Kansas river that does not flow into either the Kansas or Arkansas rivers, but directly into the Missouri River. The area drained by a river or a river system is known as its *basin*. All of Kansas is in the drainage basin of the Mississippi River. The Arkansas River flows directly into the Mississippi River in the state of Arkansas. Both the Kansas and the Marais des Cygnes rivers flow into the Missouri River which in turn empties

The Arkansas River in Wichita. The Arkansas River flows across southwestern and south central Kansas before turning southward and crossing the Oklahoma border. The river passes near many towns and cities and flows through Wichita, as is shown here.

Kansas Industrial Development Commission

into the Mississippi River north of St. Louis.

The water from the southern part of the state drains into the Arkansas either directly or through long tributaries. *Tributaries* are rivers and creeks that flow into the principal river. The large western tributary of the Arkansas that flows across southwestern Kansas is the Cimarron. Its source is in northeastern New Mexico. Here some of the tributaries to the Cimarron are mountain streams that receive some of their waters from the melting snows of the Rocky Mountains. Rattlesnake Creek, Chikaskia River, and Pawnee River are also important sources of

water in the western Arkansas River drainage basin.

Like most rivers that flow across the Great Plains, the Arkansas and the Cimarron are sand choked. The water usually carries much sediment and has a reddish color. When the rivers are in flood, they carry and move large amounts of sand by shifting it and moving it across the river bottom. Sometimes they build islands and sand bars during one flood and destroy them during the next. During the dry season there may be little or no water at all in them. The wind often shifts the sand about and builds dunes along the banks.

These rivers are sometimes said to be in old age. Their channels are filled with sand, often thirty to forty feet deep. This causes the water to move slowly. The river moves about the country and forms large curves that are called *meanders*. Near the rivers there are sometimes horseshoe-shaped lakes where old meanders were left when the river straightened itself by cutting across the narrow neck of one of these curves. The banks of the river may have a gentle slope and often a part of the river bed is overgrown with trees and brush.

The principal eastern tributaries of the Arkansas are the Verdigris and Neosho rivers. These streams are much shorter than the western tributaries. Their sources are in Kansas and Missouri and they flow south instead of east. These rivers differ greatly from the western ones. They are not sand-choked, their banks usually are steep, and in most places they are not broad and flat. The area through which these rivers flow has many trees. This causes the shorter streams flowing into them to be fairly clear. Thus, the main streams are considerably clearer than the western tributaries. The Verdigris and the Neosho flow into the Arkansas River near Muskogee, Oklahoma.

The Kansas River is a short stream in the northeastern part of the state. It forms at Junction City where the Republican River joins the Smoky Hill River. From that point the Kansas River flows eastward to its union with the Missouri River at Kansas City. The Kansas River is important because of the vast amount of water it carries, especially during flood times. Both the

Smoky Hill and Republican rivers have their headwaters in Colorado. The South Fork of the Republican River crosses Cheyenne County, Kansas, and flows northeastward into Nebraska where it joins the North Fork. The Republican, after flowing eastward across southern Nebraska, re-enters Kansas in the northeastern corner of Jewell County. The Smoky Hill River enters Wallace County from Colorado and flows in a general easterly direction. It is the deepest of the Kansas rivers. Two long tributaries, the Saline and Solomon rivers, flow into the Smoky Hill in Saline and Dickinson counties. The Big Blue River is the principal tributary to the Kansas River proper.

The Missouri River forms the northeastern boundary of the state. Although the Missouri does not flow through any part of Kansas, it is of importance to the state, especially to Kansas City, Leavenworth, and Atchison, for possible water transportation.

Most cities of Kansas are located on one of the major streams of the state. Thus, the influence of streams upon the early settlement in Kansas was great. Streams to these early communities often meant (1) a source of water for household use; (2) a means of water transportation; (3) a more level route for overland transportation by wagon and railroad along the floodplains; (4) more fertile land for a prosperous agricultural settlement; and (5) a possible source of fish for food. Names of some cities reflect their locations. For example, Junction City is located at the junction of the Smoky Hill and Republican rivers where they join to form the Kaw or Kansas River.

Flood Damage Caused by the Kaw River in Kansas City. Floods can cause much damage to good farm land and destroy much property. In 1951 the Kaw River had one of its greatest floods. At this time the Kansas City stockyards were completely flooded.

Lakes

Most of the lakes of Kansas are artificial. They have formed where large dams have been built across rivers, causing water to collect behind them. The four largest lakes at present (1959) are the result of dams constructed by the Federal and state governments. Cedar Bluff Dam and Kanopolis Dam were both built across the Smoky Hill River (Plate A). Kirwin Dam was built across the North Fork of the Solomon River and Webster Dam was constructed across the South Fork of the Solomon. When Tuttle Creek Dam on the Big Blue River north of Manhattan is closed, it will be the largest dam and will form the largest lake in the state. Cheyenne Bottoms, however, is not a man-made lake. It was formed by natural damming due to shifting of the Arkansas River in Barton County. Recent man-made damming, however, has helped to maintain a constant water level in the lake. In addition to these Federal-state reservoirs, there are thirty-nine state lakes such as Lake McKinney, near Lakin in Kearny County, and the

18

Woodson County State Park near Yates Center. Numerous smaller city and county lakes are located in various parts of the state.

The larger Kansas lakes were built to help control floods. Kanopolis Dam was built for this purpose. This dam holds back water on the Smoky Hill River. Although a large lake has been formed, the lake basin is not permitted to fill completely. Thus, when the river has a flood, the extra water can be held in the lake. Through a series of controls, a regular amount of water is permitted to flow downstream. By controlling the amount of water flowing from the lake, floods can be lessened and may even be prevented below the dam. This aids the people living along the river, since they can now use land near the river, knowing that in all probability it will not be flooded.

The lakes of Kansas have many uses. Some of the larger cities and towns in eastern Kansas get their water supply from small lakes built for that purpose. The water back of Cedar Bluff Dam may be used for irrigation of the land along the north side of the lake. The area below Kirwin Dam may be irrigated by water from Lake Kirwin. These lakes serve the farmers of their area by supplying water when it is most needed during the dry season. Other lakes are also being constructed for this purpose.

The purpose for which many people use lakes directly is recreation. People like to swim, or fish, or go boating, or just enjoy a picnic on the lake shore. Many Kansas lakes have good beaches, and tourist cabins have been built near them. The fact that a lake is used for flood control, water supply, irrigation, or power does not prevent its being used for recreation also.

There are now more than forty-eight lakes covering at least 100 acres each.

Kansas Industrial Development Commission

Fall River Dam, located in Southeast Kansas. Most of the lakes of Kansas are artificial. The larger lakes were formed where either the state or Federal Government, or both, built a large dam across a river.

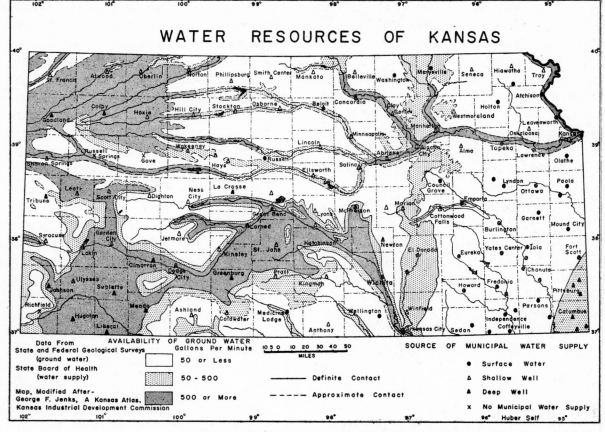

Map 4. Water Resources of Kansas

The largest of these at present, is Cedar Bluff Reservoir that has a total of 6,600 acres or about ten square miles. Many lakes and ponds of less than 100 acres have been built by farmers and ranchers for varied uses on their farms and ranches.

Ground Water

It has been estimated that one third of the water that falls to the earth as rain, snow, hail, or sleet sinks into the ground to become ground water. The amount which will soak into the ground varies from time to time and from place to place, depending upon the time of the year and the surface of the earth. More water will sink in on flat land and soft surfaces than on sloping and hard surfaces. More will probably sink in during the summer when vegetation prevents the water from running off rapidly and the ground is not frozen on top as it may be in winter.

The most important geographic influence of ground water is that cities, towns, villages, and farm homes located away from streams and springs can, by digging a well, get a supply of fresh water. Many farmers also dig wells and use the water to irrigate crops where the rainfall is scanty.

Large supplies of ground water can be obtained in many parts of Kansas (Map 4). In the Arkansas River Valley, the valley of the Kansas River, and in many counties in the western part of the state, the wells can supply over

20

500 gallons of water per minute, even though in some areas the supply of surface water is limited.

Ground water is more plentiful in western than in eastern Kansas because the rock layers in the western part of the state are young. They have not yet become so highly compacted and cemented. The pores in the rock are large, somewhat like the pore space in a sponge. Thus, they are said to have high *porosity*. Often the water contained in such pore space can flow freely from pore to pore so the rock layers are said to have high *permeability*. The nature of the rock layers, and the sand and gravel layers, in western Kansas allow that part of the state to retain much of the relatively small amount of precipitation that falls there. In eastern Kansas the rocks are older and more highly compacted and cemented. The pore space is too small for rapid permeability. In some rock layers there is practically no pore space. Some stream valleys in eastern Kansas, however, contain layers of gravel that are highly permeable and furnish much ground water.

Near Meade is an area known as Artesian Valley. In this area, which is about forty miles long and from five to fifteen miles wide, over 300 wells have been dug into the artesian basin. An artesian basin may be formed if a slanting layer of sand or sandstone lies between two layers of clay, one directly above the sand and one directly below, so that the sand or sandstone becomes a natural storage tank for water. Such a layer of sandstone holding water is called an *aquifer*. The only way to get water from such a natural tank is to drill a well into it. The layer of sand or sandstone gets its water from wherever the sand or sandstone comes to the surface and catches the water that falls onto it or runs into it. Wells drilled into such an aquifer are called *artesian* wells. If the water pressure in the aquifer is great, water will flow up and out of the well. If the pressure is not great the water has to be pumped. Most of the water in Artesian Valley comes to the surface without being pumped and is used for the irrigation of many different kinds of crops.

STUDENT ACTIVITIES

1. Draw a large map of Kansas. On it draw the Arkansas, Republican, Smoky Hill, Neosho, and other large rivers. Print the name of each river by it. Draw in five large lakes and identify them.

2. Make a list of ten different uses of water. Compare your list with the lists made by your classmates.

3. Where does your community get its water supply?

4. What are the chief uses of the rivers of Kansas? Are any used for navigation?

5. Why is ground water so important in Kansas? What is ground water? Why does western Kansas have more ground water than eastern Kansas?

6. Are there any deep wells in your community? How deep are they dug?

7. Are there many farm ponds in your community? Why are farm ponds of great importance to the farmer?

8. Which two rivers of Kansas do you believe to be the most important? Why? What cities are located along these rivers?

9. Collect pictures of the rivers and lakes of Kansas. Put them on the bulletin board for your classmates to see. Discuss the ways in which they are alike and the ways in which they differ.

10. What does each of the following terms mean?

    a. meander

    b. porosity

    c. flood plain

    d. permeability

    e. reservoir

    f. aquifer

    g. artesian well

    h. tributary

11. Name the five largest rivers of Kansas. Where is the source of each? Into what does each flow?

12. What must be done to the Missouri River to make it of greater value to the people of Kansas?

13. In what ways do the rivers of western Kansas differ from those in the eastern part of the state? Why do they differ?

14. In what ways have the rivers helped in the development of the state? How have they hindered development in some areas?

15. Should more artificial lakes be formed in Kansas? If so, why? If not, why not?

Chapter 4

REGIONS OF KANSAS

There are many contrasts between the different parts of Kansas. Some parts are rolling plains, some are rough hill lands, and yet other parts have deep valleys and flat-topped mesas. The differences in the surface of the land are caused by the action of weathering and erosion upon the different kinds and types of rocks in the area. The rocks that are very hard erode slowly and may develop into an area of ridges and hills. The softer rocks erode more rapidly, forming valleys or rolling plains.

Within Kansas are parts of three large natural regions of the United States (Map 5). A *natural region* is an area having many features of one particular kind. For example, one area may be called a region because it has many long ridges, and another will form a region because it is a rolling plain. In most cases the boundaries between regions are not sharply drawn lines as shown on maps. In many places such definite boundaries cannot be drawn since one region gradually changes into another. On the earth the boundaries are usually zones.

The Central Lowlands and the Great Plains that extend into Kansas can be better understood by studying the subregions of each (Table 1). Each subregion has certain characteristics that make it differ from every other subregion. The part of the Ozark Plateau that extends into Kansas, however, is so small that it does not need to be divided.

TABLE 1
NATURAL REGIONS OF KANSAS

REGION	SUBREGION	CHARACTERISTICS
Ozark Plateau		Rolling and hilly area that is a part of the Springfield Plain of Missouri
Central Lowland	Cherokee Plain	Hilly to rolling plain with many wooded areas; land slopes to the west about 10 feet per mile
	Chautauqua Hills	Hilly region in which the principal vegetation is grass
	Osage Cuestas	Hilly to rolling area with a series of cuestas that extend in a northeast-southwest direction; hills are grassy pasture land
	Glaciated Region	Much like the Osage Cuesta except that cuestas have been worn smooth by glaciation, or land about them has been covered by glacial material
	Flint Hills	Most rugged, hilly area in state; hills covered with grass; good pasture land; limestone cliffs
Great Plains	Wellington Plain	Rolling plains area; reddish colored soils
	Red Hills	Hilly area with much stream erosion; many buttes and mesas that are capped with gypsum; natural bridges and sink holes
	Great Bend Prairie	Flat to rolling area; some parts are poorly drained; sand dunes along the rivers
	Smoky Hills	Rough, hilly area with much stream erosion; short grass chief vegetation
	High Plains	Largest area in state; rolling plains covered with short grass and bunch grass; sand dunes along some streams; long rivers flowing generally eastward

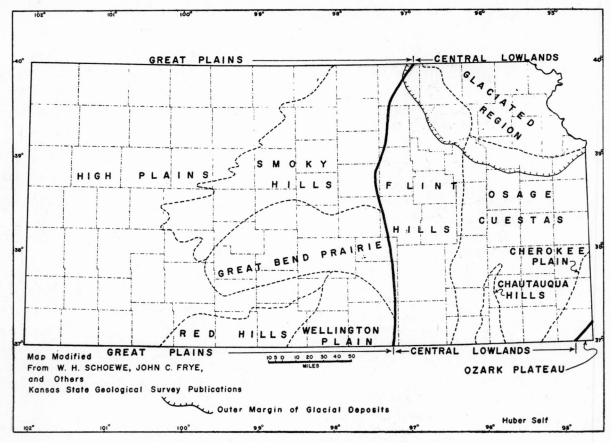

Map 5. Physiographic Map of Kansas

Ozark Plateau

The Ozark Plateau is the smallest of the natural provinces of Kansas. It is located in the southeastern corner of the state where Kansas borders Missouri and Oklahoma. The Kansas part of the plateau is a westward extension of the subregion in Missouri known as the Springfield Plain.

Although this region has no subregions in Kansas, and covers an area of only about fifty square miles, it is a very important one in the life of the state. Here are great mines from which lead and zinc ores are taken. The great piles of *chat* (waste) that remain near some of the mines are common sights. Mining is not as im-

portant today as formerly. Grazing and the dairy industry are developing. Baxter Springs and Galena are the principal cities of this region.

Central Lowlands

The Central Lowlands of eastern Kansas are a part of the great Central Lowlands province of the interior part of the United States. In general the province is an area of rolling plains and hills. In Kansas the Central Lowlands province is divided into the regions known as the Cherokee Plain, Chautauqua Hills, Osage Cuestas, Glaciated Region, and Flint Hills.

The *Cherokee Plain* is located in the southeastern part of the state just

24

north and west of the Ozark Plateau (Map 5). This region covers about 1,000 square miles and is a hilly plain which slopes westward. Local relief is not great; thus most of the hills are not high above the surrounding plain. One of the outstanding features of the region is the flat-topped Timbered Hills, almost eight miles north of Baxter Springs. They have a height of about eighty feet above the surrounding plain. Most of the rivers flowing through the region have valleys that are wide and flat. Spring and Neosho are the two principal rivers draining the area.

The Cherokee Plain is a very productive part of Kansas. It is important for both its mineral and agricultural products. Especially is the region noted for its coal production. Coal mining started about 1865. Much coal is now mined by the open pit method since the coal is near the surface. After the layer of soil has been scraped off the coal and piled alongside the pit, the coal is scooped out by great shovels. One of the common sights of the region is the long rows of material that have been formed where mining has taken place. After the coal is taken out of the ground the great trenches usually fill with water. In some places the land is being reclaimed by scraping off the tops of these ridges and planting them with fruit trees. Coal dumps are not places of beauty if left to grow up in weeds and brush. However, by landscaping, they can be made useful and beautiful homesites.

Many other minerals are also mined in the region. Much oil is produced. Sandstone and limestone are both mined and used for construction purposes. Clay, taken from pits in the region, is used in making brick, pottery, and tile.

Several different kinds of crops are grown on the Cherokee Plain. Corn, oats, hay, winter wheat, and soybeans

Kansas Industrial Development Commission

A Reclamation Lake near Pittsburg. Much of the coal mined in the Cherokee Plain comes from strip mines. After the mines are abandoned, long troughs that fill with water are left. The soil which formerly covered the coal is piled along the side of the trough and forms low rounded hills.

Osage Cuestas. The Osage Cuestas form a series of east-facing escarpments separated by rolling plains. This scene is in the central part of Wabaunsee County.

are the most important. The region is usually classed as a great farming area. In such an area the farmer may raise many kinds of crops and also keep livestock. Many farms are classed as cash grain farms since they produce grain crops chiefly to sell.

Pittsburg, Fort Scott, and Columbus are the largest cities in the region. Each has some manufacturing activity and each is also important as a distribution center for agricultural products and goods needed by the people living in the region. Chetopa, Oswego, and Arma are important smaller trading centers.

The *Chautauqua Hills* form a small region that extends southward from the southwestern part of Woodson County to the Kansas-Oklahoma border. This hill region is made up largely of thick sandstones. These sandstones have been eroded into a series of low hills that cause this region to be different from the Osage Cuestas Region which surrounds it. The Chautauqua Hills are crossed by the Verdigris, Fall, and Elk rivers which flow between steep bluffs of sandstone. Many of the low hills are covered by oak trees.

Caney is the largest of the towns in the region. All others are small distribution centers. The chief activities within the region are general farming and ranching.

The *Osage Cuestas* form the largest region in the Central Lowlands part of Kansas. It is also one of the most important regions of the state. The region is very productive, being noted not only for its agricultural products and livestock but also for the many minerals mined. The region is the most densely populated part of Kansas.

The Osage Cuestas Region is characterized by a series of eighteen cuestas which extend in a northeast-southwest direction. These *cuestas* form irregular rows of hills that have steep eastern sides and gently sloping western sides. They were caused by erosion after the sedimentary layers of limestone and shale had been tilted during the formation of the earth. The limestone, being harder than the shale, does not erode as rapidly and remains standing as a hill. The eastern front, which has heights of from fifty to 200 feet, forms such a steep slope that it is called an *escarpment*. The larger streams in the

26

region are the Neosho and the Verdigris that flow south and southeast into Oklahoma, and the Marais des Cygnes that flows east into Missouri. Usually there is a narrow timbered area along the streams.

Livestock raising and general farming are important activities in the region. In general the hills are covered with grass and are used for pasture lands. Most of the valleys are cultivated. Corn, winter wheat, oats, hay, and soybeans are important crops. The region has many fine farms, beautiful farmsteads, and good livestock.

The Osage Cuestas Region is noted for the number of minerals mined. All three of the mineral fuels—coal, petroleum, and natural gas—are produced. Asphalt rock is quarried in Bourbon and Linn counties. Limestone, the principal product used in making cement, is mined in several parts of the region. All but one of the Portland cement plants in Kansas are located in the Osage Cuestas.

Chanute, Coffeyville, Emporia, Independence, Ottawa, and Parsons are the principal cities of the region. Each has a population of over 10,000 persons. All of these cities have some manufacturing activities and each serves as the distribution center for its area. Many good highways and several railroads connect the cities and towns of this region with the other parts of Kansas.

The *Glaciated Region* is located in the northeastern corner of the state. This region differs from the other regions of Kansas in that twice during past geologic ages it has been covered by glaciers. *Glaciers*, which are large bodies of snow and ice, built up under unusually cold conditions in Canada, Alaska, and the North Pole area. These large bodies of snow and ice then

State Geological Survey of Kansas

A Glaciated Region in Northeastern Kansas. The glaciers that covered parts of northeastern Kansas left a rolling, hilly landscape. This glacial deposit, known as glacial till, is partly responsible for the richness of the area as farm land. This scene is south of Atchison in Atchison County.

pushed southward into the United States about as far as the Ohio and Missouri rivers. Two of these glaciers, one of which is now referred to as the Kansan, crossed the Missouri River and overflowed into the state (Map 5). Actually the outer edge of the glaciers and the glacial outwash extended beyond the Glaciated Region in the Osage Cuestas and the Flint Hills.

Glaciers move very, very slowly. They push large boulders and tiny rocks before them. Due to their great weight they gouge out areas of softer rocks. Dirt and other materials that become mixed with the ice may be carried many hundreds of miles from the place where it was formed. As the earth warmed, the glaciers melted and dropped the material they were carrying. Heavy deposits of this material, called *glacial debris*, were then left covering the land. Thus, in the Glaciated Region much of the surface is covered with glacial transported materials. If this glaciated material were to be removed from the surface, the uncovered area would not differ greatly from the Osage Cuestas. In places not covered by glacial debris the surface was worn smooth by the glaciers as they moved over them. In certain areas the surface of the Glaciated Region is very rough and hilly. Especially is this true for the area along the banks of the Missouri River. Sometimes this area along the Missouri is called the "Switzerland of Kansas."

The Glaciated Region is a rich agricultural area. Corn, wheat, hay, and oats are the common crops. Fruit, of which apples are the most important, is produced in large quantities. Livestock feeding is also important. Here the animals are fattened and made ready for butchering instead of being permitted to feed on the range. Many of these animals are marketed at the nearby packing plants.

Kansas City, Topeka, Lawrence, and Leavenworth are the largest cities in the region and among the largest cities in the state. All have populations of more than 25,000 persons. Kansas City, Leavenworth, and Atchison are located along the banks of the Missouri River. Lawrence and Topeka are near the Kansas River. All are connected by good highway and railway routes. Each is an important distribution center not only for the region but for the state as a whole.

The *Flint Hills* form the dividing zone between the High Plains and the Central Lowlands. This eastern boundary is determined by a very rocky escarpment several hundred feet high. The eastern edge of the region forms the most rugged surface in the state. In some places the local relief is greater than 300 feet. The land west of the east-facing escarpment varies from level to rolling, and in some places it is very hilly. A part of the northern section of the region has been glaciated.

There are many streams and rivers in this region but only one, the Kansas River, flows completely across it. The Arkansas, Blue, Neosho, Verdigris, and Marais des Cygnes rivers flow across part of the Flint Hills, and some have at least a part of their source in the region. Several of the smaller creeks and streams have been dammed so that numerous ponds and small lakes can be found in all parts of the region.

The region is the center for many mineral activities. Both petroleum and

28

The Flint Hills Region in Kansas. The Flint Hills is one of the most important ranching regions in Kansas. These hills have developed in an area of weather-resistant flinty limestone. Most of the land is gently rolling, but in many places there are steep slopes. This scene is located in the west central part of Elk County.

natural gas are produced. Helium was first taken from a gas well near Dexter. The Fort Riley and Cottonwood limestones, two of the state's most important building stones, are quarried in several different locations.

The Flint Hills form one of the most beautiful regions of Kansas. Its hilly surface is covered with bluestem, one of the best grasses for cattle to graze upon. So thick is this grass that the region is sometimes called the Bluestem Region. Caring for livestock is the chief type of farming. Many thousands of cattle are shipped into the region each year from Oklahoma, Texas, and other states. They graze upon the rich grasses of the ranches and farms as they are being fattened for market. Because of the livestock industry, Abilene became a famous "cow town" almost 100 years ago. It became the first great market for Texas Longhorn cattle when the first railroad extended west to the town.

Arkansas City, El Dorado, Junction City, Manhattan, and Winfield are the largest cities in the region, all having populations of over 12,000. Many important smaller cities such as Abilene, Augusta, Clay Center, Herington, and Marysville also contribute much to the region. All are important distribution and shopping centers and most have manufacturing activities of some kind.

Great Plains

The Great Plains province is one of the large physical regions of the United States. It extends northward from southwestern Texas through the states just east of the Rocky Mountains and into Canada. This large province is characterized by rolling plains, broken hill lands, and grass. Except along stream valleys, very few trees will be found. In Kansas the Great Plains are divided into the Smoky Hills, Great Bend Prairie, Wellington Plain, Red Hills, and High Plains.

The *Wellington Plain* is a small region located in the south central part of the state. For the most part this region is a rolling plain that varies in elevation from about 1,000 to 1,300 feet. In some places the harder rocks have formed ledges along the hillsides. Drainage from the region is through the tributaries of the Arkansas River. Most of the land in the Wellington Plain is under cultivation. The reddish colored soils are fertile and produce good crops of wheat, grain sorghums, and hay. Petroleum and natural gas are the chief minerals. Anthony, Caldwell, and Wellington are the principal cities.

The *Red Hills Region*, sometimes called the Cimarron Breaks Area, borders the Wellington Plain on the west. It differs greatly from its eastern neighbor in that it is a very hilly area. Many of the hills have flat, table-like tops. The hills are the result of differences in the hardness of rocks. The gypsum that covers the tops of some of the hills does not erode as rapidly as the softer shales and sandstones. A large flat-topped hill is called a *mesa*,

the smaller ones are called *buttes*. Also found in the region is a natural bridge near Sun City; St. Jacobs Well, a sink hole in Clark County; and Big Basin, a depression about a mile across and a hundred feet deep, also located in Clark County. The Red Hills are often said to be the most scenic region in Kansas. The region gets its name from the red color of the exposed rocks and soils. The Cimarron is the only river of importance, but the many tributaries cause breaks in the landscape.

There are many good farms and several large ranches in the Red Hills. Wheat is the chief crop, but grain sorghums and hay crops are also important. Medicine Lodge, with a population of about 2,500 people, is the largest city. The smaller towns and villages are important only as local trading centers.

The *Great Bend Prairie* is dominated by the large northward bend of the Arkansas River. This region is mainly one of flat lands, often so flat that

State Geological Survey of Kansas

In the Red Hills. In the Red Hills are many flat-topped hills called buttes. Many buttes like this are located in the vicinity of Sun City in Barber County.

they are poorly drained. The rivers have broad flat beds through which the streams wind in many channels. In several places along the banks sand-dunes have been formed. Where drainage is poor there may be swampy areas. In Barton County is a low area about nine miles long and seven miles wide called Cheyenne Bottoms. The State Forestry, Fish, and Game Commission now controls this area and has made it into a preserve for waterfowl.

The Great Bend Prairie is rich in both agricultural and mineral resources. Good soil and level land make the farming of wheat, grain sorghums, and hay crops profitable. Oil and gas are produced in each county in the region. Salt is mined in Reno and Rice counties and clay is available for making brick. Because of the richness of the region, many large cities are located in it. Wichita, the largest city in Kansas, is an industrial center. Hutchinson, Great Bend, McPherson, and Newton are also important manufacturing and transportation centers.

The *Smoky Hills Region* is located in north central Kansas. It borders the Flint Hills on the east and the Great Bend Prairie on the south. Due to the differences in the hardness of the sandstones, limestones, and shales that make up the region, it is very hilly. Local relief is not usually great but in places it may be as much as 250 to 300 feet. Because of the hilly and rolling landscape, flat-topped hills, large sandrocks, and the smoky blue haze when the area is seen from a distance, the region is one of the most interesting in Kansas. Many tourists travel through the area each year just to look at the many natural formations.

State Geological Survey of Kansas

A Ledge of Dakota Sandstone. The ledge of Dakota sandstone is the remains of sediments deposited in the region millions of years ago. This scene is in Ellsworth County south of Terra Cotta.

Oil, gas, salt, and clay are the principal minerals of the region. It is also important for its crops of grain sorghums, wheat, and hay. In the northern part of the region, corn is an important crop. Salina is the largest city in the Smoky Hills, but both Concordia and Russell have populations of over 5,000 persons.

The *High Plains* form the largest region in Kansas as they cover more than a third of the state. The High Plains range in elevation from approximately 2,000 feet along their eastern border to over 4,000 feet along the Colorado-Kansas boundary. The High Plains in Kansas are part of the region that extends from the Panhandle of Texas, across Oklahoma and Kansas, and into Nebraska. It is believed these plains were formed by rivers depositing the material they washed from the Rocky

Mountains on top of the lower plains. In general, the region is fairly level. There are, however, areas where rivers have cut steep banks, or winds have carved rocks into peculiar forms. Monument Rock east of Elkader and Castle Rock southeast of Quinter are examples. Numerous depressions, both large and small, are scattered throughout the region. In some places the depressions are called buffalo wallows. During rainy seasons these depressions form many small lakes.

The Arkansas, Cimarron, Smoky Hill, Solomon, Saline, and Republican rivers all cross some parts of the High Plains. These rivers are all long, and usually flow in an easterly direction. Large dams such as Cedar Bluff and Kirwin have been built on some of the rivers. In places sand dunes have formed. The largest of the dune areas are in the vicinity of the Cimarron and Arkansas rivers in the southwestern corner of the state and in Hamilton, Kearny, Finney, and Gray counties.

The High Plains is a region of large farms and large ranches. Wheat is the principal crop although grain sorghums are widely grown. Cattle are found in all parts of the region. Elevators and stockyards are located in every city and in many of the towns and villages. The activities of the cities, towns, and farms are closely related. Dodge City, Garden City, Hays, Liberal, and Pratt are the largest and most important communities.

STUDENT ACTIVITIES

1. In which region and subregion is your home?

2. On a large map of Kansas draw in the regions and subregions. Draw in lines to show the location of each of the large rivers. Print in the name of each river and subregion.

3. If you traveled from Atchison to Liberal, through which subregions would you pass? From Baxter Springs to Smith Center?

4. Bring to class pictures of the various parts of Kansas. Study each picture and try to tell in which part of the state it is located. By pointing to it on the map, show where the area of each picture is located.

5. In which part of the state is the largest area of highest elevation? Lowest?

6. What is a natural region? How many natural regions has Kansas? What is the largest? The smallest?

7. How does life in the Cherokee Plain differ from life on the High Plains? Why? How do the landforms in these two regions differ? In what ways do the landforms influence what the people do to make a living?

8. Why were the streams and rivers of more importance to the pioneers than they are to the people today?

9. Have you traveled in states that border Kansas? Tell the class how the lands of Kansas differ from those of other states. In what ways are they like those of other states?

10. In which regions of the state is most of the coal mined? Most of the oil?

11. Select what you think is the most interesting region of Kansas and describe it.

Chapter 5

WEATHER AND CLIMATE

Weather and climate have a great influence upon the kind of work people do, the type of home in which they live, the kind of clothing they wear, and the food they eat. Whether or not an airplane will be permitted to fly depends upon the weather. Most daily newspapers contain weather reports, and several times during each day the radio and television announcers give reports about weather conditions. So important are weather and climate in our lives that the Federal Government has established the United States Weather Bureau.

Weather may be defined as the daily changes in the weather elements. The principal elements are temperature, rainfall, humidity, pressure, winds, sunshine, and storms. As you know, some days there will be rain, some days not. Temperature in the morning may be low and the starting of the day cool, but by afternoon the temperature may have increased and the day become hot. Sometimes the wind is strong, but at other times the air hardly moves.

In Kansas there are over 180 weather stations. Most of these stations are small, and the men or women who run them also do other work. Each of these small stations has several weather instruments. The thermometer is used to record the temperature; the barometer records the pressure of the atmosphere; the rain gauge tells how much, if any, rain has fallen; and the anemometer shows how fast the wind is blowing. Each day the person in charge of the station reads the instruments at 7:00 o'clock in the morning and 7:00 o'clock in the evening. He then sends this information to his Kansas area weather station which prepares the area forecast.

Some of the larger cities and the more important airports have large weather stations that employ many full-time workers. These people gather the information from all the other stations in Kansas. They put it together in a usable form. People at the principal weather stations in the rest of the United States are doing the same thing for their states. The Kansas weather people send their information to the other states and, in turn, receive the weather information from the other states. When the weather station has received all this information, it is entered on a map. Some of the other important Kansas stations, especially those located at large airports, also make weather maps.

The weather map is very interesting. It shows the direction in which the wind is blowing, where storms are located, how much sunshine a place has, how hot or how cold it is, how much and where it has rained, and other weather information. Because the weather is always changing, some stations make one map a day, and some two or more maps a day. By studying several of these maps, the weather forecaster is able to tell what kind of weather a place is going to have. Most of the weather changes in Kansas come

Southeastern Kansas Farm Scene in the Winter. During the winter Kansas often has heavy snows which may do harm, but the snows also help the farmer by adding moisture to the soil. This farmstead is located in southeastern Kansas.

from either the northwest or southwest. Thus, it is much more important to study weather conditions in the states north and west of Kansas than in those to the east.

Climate is defined as the composite of weather conditions over a long period of time; thus, it will include the averages as well as the extremes. The person interested in climate also wants to know about temperature, wind, rain, and all the other weather elements, but he wants to know what they have been for several years. For example, the person studying climate is more interested in the total amount of rain that falls at a station during a year than the amount that falls in any one day. When he has this information for several years he finds the average. He can then tell about how much rain will fall at a particular station during the year. By averaging temperature, wind speeds, amount of sunshine, and other factors he is able to state what the climate is most likely to be. This long record will also give information about possible extremes in weather conditions. Such information is of great value to the farmer, the fruit grower, and the cattle raiser. By knowing about what to expect, they can plan much of their work ahead of time. The Weather Bureau employs people who do nothing but figure climates. These people are called *climatologists*.

Elements of Weather

Temperature changes in Kansas vary greatly from day to day, from season to season, and from place to place. In general the summers are long and sometimes very hot. Winters are usually short and may be mild or very cold.

The average annual temperature for the state is 55° Fahrenheit. This is about the same as the average temperature for the states of Missouri and

Virginia. July and August are the hottest months with temperatures that average 79.2° and 78° F. However, these months may have temperatures that average as high as 87.2° or as low as 73.8° F. January is the coldest month with an average temperature of 30° F. December, January, and February may all have monthly temperatures which average below the 32° F. freezing mark. The highest average annual temperature is along the eastern part of the southern border. Here the average is about 58° F. The lowest average annual temperature, about 52° F., is in the northwestern part of the High Plains Region. Temperatures at all seasons usually average higher as one travels from the northwestern

to the southeastern part of the state.

Daily temperatures of 100° F. or higher are often recorded in various parts of the state during the summer. The highest temperature on record is 121° recorded at Fredonia and near Alton. Temperature below 0° is usually recorded somewhere in the state during the winter season. The lowest temperature on record is —40° which is 72° below freezing. This temperature was recorded at Lebanon on February 13, 1905.

The temperature extremes, that is the highest and lowest temperatures, are often of greater importance than the average temperature. When the weather is too hot, many crops will be burned by the sunshine and hot winds.

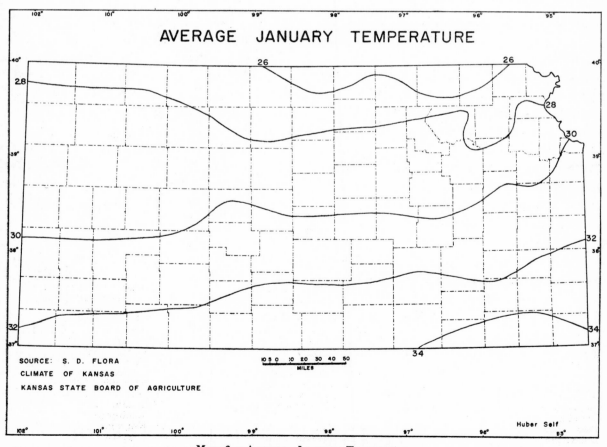

SOURCE: S. D. FLORA
CLIMATE OF KANSAS
KANSAS STATE BOARD OF AGRICULTURE

Map 6. Average January Temperature

TABLE 2

TEMPERATURES AT SELECTED STATIONS

STATION	AVERAGE HIGH TEMPERATURE	AVERAGE LOW TEMPERATURE	AVERAGE TEMPERATURE FOR YEAR
Atchison	January 28.3	July 78.6	54.3
Colby	January 28.8	July 77.2	52.4
Dodge City	January 31.1	July 79.1	54.9
Emporia	January 30.7	July 79.5	55.8
Fort Scott	January 33.1	July 79.9	57.2
Garden City	January 30.9	July 78.9	54.9
Hays	January 29.4	July 79.3	54.1
Hutchinson	January 31.0	July 80.2	56.1
Independence	January 34.8	July 80.4	58.4
Kansas City	January 30.1	July 79.8	55.5
Larned	January 30.2	July 80.2	55.6
Lawrence	January 29.9	July 79.1	55.3
Manhattan	January 29.2	July 80.2	55.3
Medicine Lodge	January 33.5	July 81.2	57.9
Norton	January 27.5	July 78.5	52.8
Phillipsburg	January 27.9	July 80.0	53.7
Salina	January 29.7	July 81.0	55.9
Topeka	January 29.4	July 79.7	55.1
WaKeeney	January 29.8	July 78.7	54.1
Wichita	January 32.1	July 80.4	56.7
Winfield	January 33.2	July 80.9	57.8

When it is too cold, the same crops will be frozen. Not only is farm work influenced by temperature, but the work of people in cities and towns is affected by it.

The *growing season* is that period of the year from spring to fall when plants can grow. The limits of the growing season are determined by killing frosts, and frost is largely determined by temperature. The growing season is often defined as that part of the year between the last killing frost in spring and the first killing frost in fall.

Not all crops grow in the same length of time. From the time field corn is planted until it is full grown and ready to harvest requires about 140 frost-free days. Thus, it is said that corn requires a growing season of about 140 days.

In Allen, Neosho, Labette, and Cherokee counties there will probably be no killing frost after April 10. The people in the northwestern part of the High

TABLE 3

TEMPERATURE EXTREMES

MONTH	LOWEST TEMPERATURE RECORDED	HIGHEST TEMPERATURE RECORDED
January	—34 Seneca, 1892	85 Liberal, 1927
February	—40 Lebanon, 1905	91 Medicine Lodge, 1904
March	—21 Ulysses, 1920	100 Hugoton, 1910
April	— 2 Oakley, 1936	103 Kiowa, 1893
May	14 Wallace, 1909	108 Ellsworth, 1939
June	30 Tribune, 1917	116 Hugoton, 1911
July	32 Tribune, 1888	121 Fredonia, 1936
August	33 St. Francis, 1910	119 Wellington, 1936
September	18 St. Francis, 1926	113 Sedan, 1939
October	— 3 Wallace, 1926	101 Wellington, 1939
November	—20 Monument, 1887	96 Kingman, 1909
December	—26 Oberlin, 1932	86 Ulysses, 1939

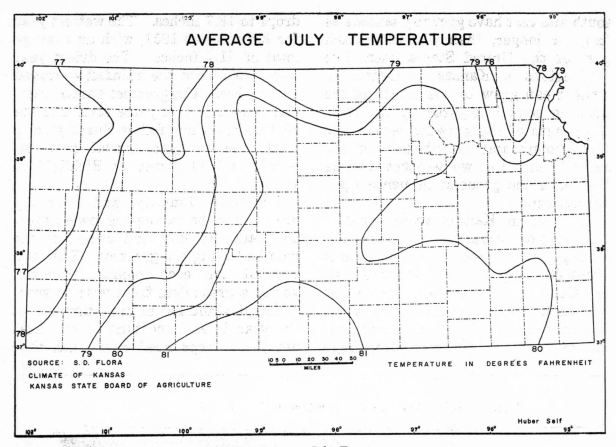

AVERAGE JULY TEMPERATURE

SOURCE: S. D. FLORA
CLIMATE OF KANSAS
KANSAS STATE BOARD OF AGRICULTURE

TEMPERATURE IN DEGREES FAHRENHEIT

Huber Self

Map 7. Average July Temperature

Plains, however, may expect to have killing frosts for at least three weeks longer, or until May 1. Places having frost latest in the spring are the places with highest elevation.

Frost comes earlier in Cheyenne and Rawlins counties than in any other part of Kansas. The southeastern part of the state will be the last area to have a killing frost.

The average length of the growing season for all parts of the state is shown on Map 8. The southeastern part of the state and the area around Kansas City have the longest growing season; the western part of the High Plains has the shortest growing season. The growing season for most of the High Plains is less than 170 days in length; in the

southeastern part of Kansas it is 195 or more days.

During the winter, or the non-growing season, there are many warm days. Frost, snow, or freezing temperatures may occur at any time, however, and will kill most crops that start to grow during the few warm days. A few hardy crops, such as winter wheat, grow all winter long. When the ground is covered with snow, or ice, or frost for any length of time it becomes frozen. The freezing may go as deep as ten to twenty inches; then the weather must be warm enough for several days to thaw the ground.

Kansas has a longer growing season than the states north of it, except those along the Pacific coast. The states

37

south and east have growing seasons as long, or longer, than Kansas. Each part of the United States, then, like the regions of Kansas, is limited in what it can grow by the length of the growing season required by the crop. The length of the growing season and the amount and distribution of the rainfall are the two weather factors that have the greatest influence upon agriculture.

Rainfall in Kansas varies greatly from east to west across the state. The average rainfall over the whole state is about 26.5 inches. However, the eastern third of the state averages about 34.5 inches per year; the central third has an average rainfall of 25.9 inches; and the western third rainfall average drops to 18.7 inches. The wettest year for Kansas was 1951, with an average total of 41.4 inches. The driest year was 1936, when the rainfall averaged 18.3 inches. The greatest annual rainfall recorded by any one station is the 65.3 inches which fell at Burlington in 1941; the smallest annual total reported is 7.09 inches at Richfield in 1935.

December, January, and February are the months having the lowest average rainfall; May and June are the months having the greatest. The total rainfall for each month, however, varies a great deal from year to year.

The distribution of rain throughout the year is as important as the total amount. Crops need rain when they

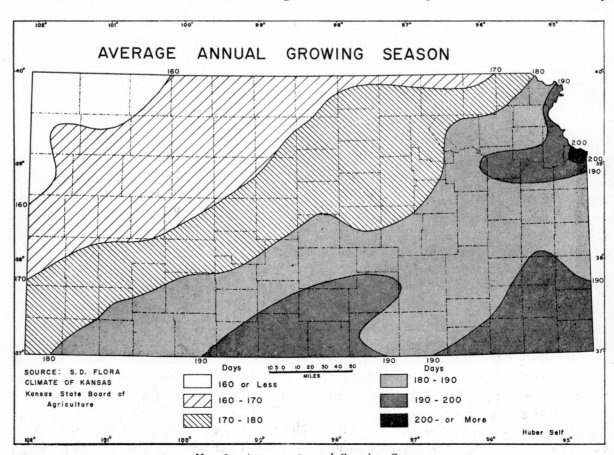

Map 8. Average Annual Growing Season

38

TABLE 4

RAINFALL OF SELECTED STATIONS

STATION	MONTH HAVING LEAST RAINFALL (AVERAGE)		MONTH HAVING HIGHEST RAINFALL (AVERAGE)		TOTAL RAINFALL FOR YEAR (AVERAGE)
Arkansas City	January	1.00	June	4.90	33.86
Atchison	January	1.03	September	4.72	34.98
Chanute	January	1.31	May	5.48	32.45
Colby	January	0.26	July	2.62	18.02
Columbus	January	1.92	June	6.04	41.86
Concordia	January	0.49	June	4.15	25.24
Dodge City	January	0.37	June	3.19	20.13
El Dorado	January	0.84	May	4.44	31.03
Elkhart	January	0.30	May	2.42	17.13
Ellsworth	January	0.64	June	4.30	26.33
Emporia	January	0.81	June	4.73	34.10
Fort Scott	December	1.56	June	5.50	39.99
Garden City	January	0.35	June	2.95	19.01
Goodland	January	0.26	June	2.77	17.98
Hays	January	0.34	June	4.09	23.05
Hutchinson	January	0.72	July	2.64	28.53
Independence	January	1.45	May	4.45	37.70
Johnson	January	0.27	June	5.28	15.85
Junction City	January	0.70	May	2.55	31.55
Kansas City	December	1.33	June	4.60	36.19
Larned	January	0.43	May	4.80	23.48
Lawrence	January	1.09	June	3.93	35.40
Liberal	January	0.29	May	4.88	18.94
Manhattan	January	0.71	May	2.87	32.03
Medicine Lodge	January	0.48	June	4.61	25.47
Newton	January	0.75	May	4.29	31.25
Phillipsburg	January	0.39	June	4.78	22.41
Pittsburg	December	1.71	June	3.67	41.65
Richfield	January	0.36	June	5.69	16.88
Russell	January	0.44	May	2.40	24.53
Salina	January	0.62	June	4.19	27.00
Scott City	January	0.36	June	4.50	18.61
Sharon Springs	January	0.19	June	2.90	16.32
Topeka	January	0.91	May	4.42	32.58
Ulysses	January	0.26	June	2.94	17.24
WaKeeney	January	0.26	May	3.07	21.54
Wichita	January	0.71	May	4.66	30.37

are growing. It is necessary, then, that there be enough water during the growing season. Some crops require more water than others. Wheat does not need as much water as corn. Parts of Kansas do not have enough rainfall to permit the raising of good crops. Some farmers irrigate, if they can, and do not depend entirely upon rainfall. In general, however, about 75 per cent of the total annual rainfall comes during the growing season.

When high temperatures exist for several weeks at a time, conditions are not favorable for rainfall. In such temperatures, the winds become hot and dry and a drought, or dry period, exists. In 1930, 1934, and 1936 Kansas had severe droughts. During these dry periods crops will not grow, so there is nothing to hold the soil in place. The winds pick up the dry soil and cause dust storms. Actually the farms may be blown away. The lack of rainfall, then, is just as bad as the excess of rain which causes floods.

Snowfall, like rainfall, is a form of moisture or precipitation. The amount of snow that falls ranges from less than ten inches per year in the south central part of the state along the Oklahoma border to over twenty-four inches per year in the northwestern counties. February and March are the months having the greatest snowfall. Over much of Kansas snow remains on the ground for only a few days.

Wind is air in motion. During much of the year the wind comes from the south. In December, January, and February, however, cold winds from the north are common. The winds are very important to us. They bring our rains. The speed with which the wind moves is called *wind velocity*. The average hourly speed of wind in Wichita throughout the year is about twelve miles per hour. The months when the wind velocity is greatest are March and April. July and August are the months when the wind velocity is lowest.

The speed of the winds is highest over flat lands that have few buildings, trees, or hills. In many ways the wind is like water. When water flows against a rock, it either stops, flows around the rock, or stores up enough water to flow over the rock. In like manner, trees, hills, and buildings act as a block to the wind and slow it down. In the eastern part of Kansas where there are more hills, trees, and buildings, the velocity of the wind is less than in the western part of the state.

Air Masses and Storms

The weather and climate, as we see them every day, are a mixture of all the weather elements at the same time. What these elements do and what they

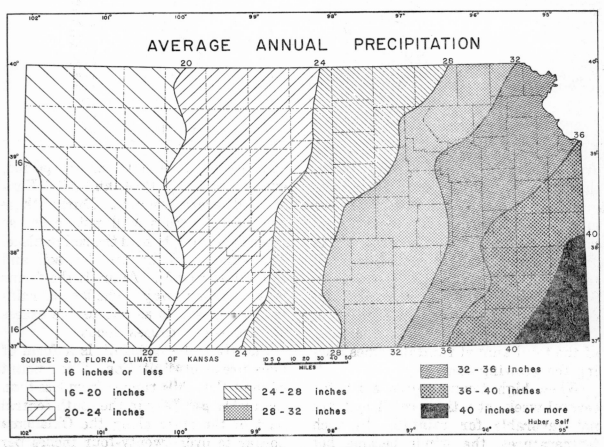

Map 9. Average Annual Precipitation

40

are like is not determined in Kansas alone. Many times during the year, and especially in winter, the weather of Kansas is greatly influenced by weather conditions in Canada, Alaska, and over the Arctic Ocean. In the warmer months, weather conditions over the Gulf of Mexico, and other parts of the country affect Kansas weather. Sometimes the long dry periods are caused by hot winds from the deserts of New Mexico and Arizona. During the winter, large masses of air settle in the Arctic Region. This air becomes cold and dense. Later, the air mass starts to move south across the plains of Canada and the United States, often extending as far south as Texas. At the same time, a mass of air may have settled over the Gulf of Mexico and may start moving north. Often these two masses meet over Kansas and the other plains states.

Air masses are known as warm air masses or cold air masses. The air mass from the Arctic will have a low temperature and, since it was formed over land, will probably have only a little moisture in it. As the air mass moves south, it is moving over ground that is warmer than the air. Since the air is colder than the ground over which it moves, it is called a cold air mass. The warm ground begins to heat the cold air, causing currents and winds in the mass. This heating action is much like the action in boiling water.

The air mass which forms over the Gulf of Mexico will be warm and have much moisture in it. As it moves north, it is known as a warm air mass, since it is warmer than the ground over which it is moving. As the air mass moves, it becomes cooled and set-

A Wind Vane and Anemometer. On top of the weather station will be seen the wind vane and the anemometer. The wind vane shows the direction from which the wind is blowing while the anemometer, on the right, indicates the speed.

tled, much as a pan of boiling water does as it cools. When these two air masses meet over Kansas, or any other place, a series of storms is caused. The line along which these two different air masses meet is called a *front*.

Most storms do much more good than harm. Storms bring rains that help the crops to grow. In summer a storm often cools the air and makes the day more pleasant. The storms that form along the fronts are called "cyclonic storms." When the cold air and warm air masses meet, the cold air, being the heavier, forces the warm air to rise.

41

Weather Instruments. The cage-like box on the right is where the thermometers are kept. They are not in the direct sun yet the wind can flow past them. The instrument on the left is a rain gauge.

As the warm air rises, it cools. As it cools it cannot hold all of its moisture; thus, the moisture falls to the ground as rain. This rain, the difference in pressure between the warm and cold air masses, and the winds that are mixing the air masses form a *cyclone*. A cyclone is not dangerous and does not damage property. As the two air masses mix, their temperatures and pressures become even and the cyclone dies.

Most of you can remember some morning in the autumn when the weather seemed ideal. The sky was clear except for a few high, fleecy clouds. The wind was blowing from the southwest just enough to move the leaves. The temperature was warm. About ten o'clock the sunshine began to disappear as dark clouds appeared on the western horizon. Soon the southwest wind was gone and everything became quiet. Then, almost all at once, the dark clouds moved overhead. The air became much cooler as the temperature dropped and rain started to fall. The wind was then strong again, but cool and blowing from the northwest. You were then in the cyclone along the front. Soon the storm moved on to the east and the sun shone again; the clouds had gone with the storm. The wind still came from the northwest and the temperature remained cool because you were then in the cold air mass.

Whether or not a cyclonic storm will develop along the front depends upon the differences in the two air masses. If there is only a small difference, a storm may not develop. Should the difference be great, then severe storms may develop and last for several hours.

The thunderstorm is another type of storm that often develops over the High Plains and eastern Kansas. Thunderstorms are local storms that occur most often in the summer and early fall, but may happen during any season. On a hot summer day the ground becomes heated, and the air, filled with moisture, starts to rise. There seems to be little or no breeze, but this is only because the air is moving upward. As the air moves skyward, it cools and the moisture condenses. Soon large *cumulo-nimbus* clouds, often called thunderheads, begin to form. They seem to have a flat base, but their tops look snowy white and seem to grow with great puffs. In the afternoon other clouds begin to appear. There is lightning and thunder. Suddenly the wind becomes strong and there is a downpour of rain. There may even be some hail. The air grows cooler. Suddenly the rain stops and the storm is over.

The thunderstorm may be a great help to the farmers. It may bring rain at the exact time it is needed. The most dangerous part of the thunderstorm is the lightning.

The *tornado* is the most dangerous and destructive storm that occurs in Kansas. This storm is the one that many people call a cyclone because they do not understand how cyclonic storms are formed. Texas, Kansas, and Iowa have more tornadoes than the other states. Tornadoes have occurred in all parts of Kansas. In general, the storms move from the southwest toward the northeast.

Tornadoes may occur during any month, at any time of the day or night. They are most common, however, in the months of May and June. The months in which tornadoes are least likely to appear are December and January.

The tornado is a very severe and usually small storm. It may develop along a front where the air masses have their greatest differences. Many heavy, dark thunderclouds gather and there is a strong wind. From the center of the storm, a funnel of whirling wind drops. In the middle of the funnel there is almost a vacuum. When the funnel strikes buildings, trees, or other things in its path, there is a breaking, snapping, and tearing as bricks, fences, or walls are torn apart and scattered. Windows and walls of houses are blown out and up because the air within the house is more dense and presses outward toward the vacuum as it passes. The tornado is a fast worker. It is believed that winds near the center may blow at the rate of 200 to 300 miles per hour. The storm may move along its path at the rate of twenty to forty miles per hour. The path, however, is not wide. Usually it is a quarter of a mile or less in width, and not more than five to ten miles in length.

Each Kansas citizen should be prepared to protect himself when a tornado strikes. Many people have storm cellars.

A Tornado in Action. The most dangerous of all storms is the tornado. This tornado occurred about three miles west of Manhattan in May, 1949.

Huber Self

STUDENT ACTIVITIES

1. What is the difference between weather and climate?

2. Keep a record for a month of the weather at your school. Each morning at 9:00 o'clock record the temperature, wind direction, whether it is cloudy or clear, if it is raining, and the changes from the day before.

3. Study the maps in this chapter and see what they record for your home community.

4. What is the relationship between the length of the growing season and the kind of crops planted?

5. How does the temperature in the eastern part of Kansas differ from that in the western part of the state? What is the difference in rainfall?

6. What does each of the following terms mean?
   a. wind   e. isotherm
   b. water vapor   f. growing season
   c. precipitation   g. tornado
   d. isohyet   h. cyclone

7. How does the weather in your community differ from day to day? How does the climate differ from season to season?

8. What instrument is used to measure rainfall?

9. What places have recorded the lowest temperatures in the state? The lowest amount of rainfall? The highest temperatures? The highest rainfall? Is there a relationship between rainfall and temperature?

10. What is the length of the growing season in your community? What are the chief crops of your area? How does your area differ from that of Sherman County? Crawford County?

11. Why is the study of weather and climate important? In what ways is the weather and climate of Kansas related to the weather and climate of the nation?

12. Make a collection of pictures about storms and clouds. Use a reference book to find the correct name for each cloud. Post your pictures on the bulletin board.

13. Write the office of the United States Weather Bureau nearest your home and ask for some copies of the daily weather map published. Study a series of the maps and note the direction most storms move across the state and nation.

14. Talk to several farmers or business men in your community about the effect of the weather on their business. Write a paper about what you are told, then discuss it with your classmates.

15. Have you ever seen a tornado? Have you ever seen the area over which a tornado has passed? Describe what you saw to the rest of the class.

Chapter 6

SOILS AND THEIR CONSERVATION

The soil is the earth's most valuable resource. Most of man's food, clothing, and shelter comes either directly or indirectly from the soil. Plant life in general depends directly on the soil for its growth. Animals depend directly on plants or on other animals for their existence. Man, in turn, depends on plants and animals for his food and many other necessities.

The soil of Kansas is of primary importance to the state. It is the greatest natural resource of Kansas. For us to know the soil and how to care for it is of extreme importance. If the soil is used properly, it will last indefinitely. Some soils in England have been used for more than 1,000 years and are now more productive than in any earlier time. On the other hand, soil can easily be damaged or destroyed.

Soil Formation

The forming of soil is a complex process. Many factors are included in it. The kind of rock broken down, the amount of rainfall, conditions of temperature, slope of the land, kind of plant life, length of time, and other factors are all important in forming soils.

Soils are made up primarily of fine particles of rock to which has been added decayed plant and animal life. Most soils are largely of rock materials. Plants and animals grow and die on or near the surface and their remains become a part of the soil. Many tiny plants and animals and some larger ones, as earthworms, live in the soil

and aid in its formation. The decayed plant and animal life is called *humus*, or organic matter. This element is also a very important part of soil.

Soil-forming processes are active from the surface of the earth down to solid rock. The forming of soil goes on very slowly. A hundred or even a thousand years may be required to form one inch of soil. The materials completely formed into soil are, in many places, only a few inches thick. Most soils are more than 90 per cent rock particles.

As soils form they tend to develop layers, or zones. A cross-section showing these bands is called the *soil profile*. These profiles can easily be seen, in many cases, along the edges of freshly cut ditches or in cuts along highways. The profile may show a different number of zones, but it commonly shows three. These zones, beginning at the surface, are called A, B, and C horizons. The A horizon, or top soil, is the darker top zone from which soil materials may be removed by ground water. Some of the materials carried by ground water are dissolved while others are tiny particles. Some are carried out through the soil and some downward. This process of removing soil substances is called *leaching*. The B horizon, or subsoil, is the second, lighter-colored zone in which the down-moving particles lodge. In some parts of Kansas the B horizon gets so filled with these tiny particles that water does not move freely in it. This zone is then classed as "hardpan" or "claypan." The C horizon extends

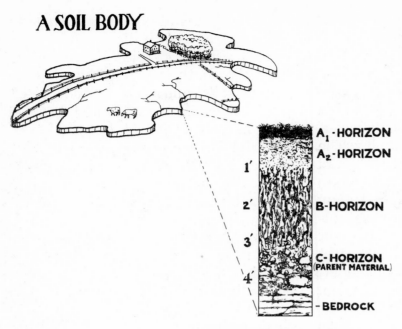

A SOIL BODY

A₁-HORIZON
A₂-HORIZON

1'

2' B-HORIZON

3'

C-HORIZON
(PARENT MATERIAL)

4'

- BEDROCK

A Soil Profile. The formation of soil is one of the most important processes of nature. Note that the A-1 horizon is where the plants live and along with the A-2 horizon is where they get most of their food.

A SOIL PROFILE

Wisconsin Geological and Natural History Survey

downward from the B horizon. It is not changed by the ground water. The A and B horizons are of great importance to the farmer. The A horizon is depended upon chiefly for growing crops. The B horizon is more closely related to moisture conditions except in case of deep-rooting plants. This compact layer may prevent free movement of moisture into the soil or to growing plants but is favorable for holding water in farm ponds.

Variety in color is one of the most noticeable things about soils. It has long been observed that grasslands tend to have dark soils and forested lands gray soils. A cause of this difference is that grassland soils contain more humus than soils under forest cover. The dark color comes from the stain, or dye, of plant life, similar to that in coffee or tea. The red color in soils is from iron rust (oxide). In hot, rainy lands the iron in the soil rusts freely and gives the soils a dark red color. In colder lands the iron does not rust so much which makes the soil only light red or yellowish. In Kansas, the red effect is moderate. It develops largely beneath the topsoil where the dark humus is not plentiful. In general where the soils show red, the surface materials have been eroded away.

Classes of Soils

Many things are included in classifying soils. Size of soil particles, color of soils, position where found, and plant foods in the soil are conditions commonly considered.

Soil may be divided into two general classes—one that has lime in the soil, the other without lime. In rather rainy areas the lime is dissolved and carried out of the soil. Under low rainfall the lime remains in the soil. Rainfall in parts of eastern Kansas is plentiful enough that some of the soil has

47

lost most of the lime. That is the reason why some farmers use large quantities of ground limestone on their lands.

Soils may be grouped into four classes according to size of particles, with several subdivisions. Soil composed of very fine particles is classed as clay. The slightly coarser particles make silt, and so on through the coarser materials to the sandy soils, gravelly soils, and stony soils. Mixtures of these form yet another class of soil. Thus, a mixture of clay and sand is called loam. If most of the material is clay, it is a clay loam; if most of it is sand, a sandy loam. Other mixtures may be silt loam or gravelly loam.

Sometimes soils are classified according to the position they occupy. If a soil remains where it is formed, it is called *residual soil*. If a soil has been moved to another place, it is called *transported soil*. Transported soils may be subdivided. Those carried by water are *alluvial soils*, those carried by wind are *aeolian soils*, and those moved by ice, *glacial soils*. If the aeolian material is very fine, it is called *loess*. Loessal material is so fine that much of it is carried long distances. In the southern High Plains there are many areas of residual soil for the soil is still in the place where it was formed. All three kinds of transported soils can be found within the state. Along the valleys of the rivers, and where the rivers overflow, alluvial soil can be found. Glacial soils are to be found in the Glaciated Region, as much of the soil was pushed into the region by the great glaciers. Along the banks of the Missouri River and the northwestern High Plains are large deposits of loess.

Soil Conservation Service

Prairie Forest Soil. A soil profile located about 1.5 miles south of Garnett on the United States Highway No. 169. Note that the topsoil—the A Horizon—above the stick is twenty to twenty-four inches thick.

The Chinese Road in Doniphan
County. This road has been built
through an area of loessal soil. Notice the steep vertical banks. Roads
built through such areas as this are
common in parts of northern China.

Soils are frequently referred to by
color. Some accept black or dark soils
as being fertile and red soils as being
poor. Such references are misleading
because color is not a good key to soil
fertility. Some black soils are fertile,
some poor. Some red soils are fertile,
some poor. More often, however, the
dark soils are fertile and the red and
yellow soils poor.

Soil Regions

Over broad zones of the earth the soil
formation factors act in such a way
that the soils throughout an area are
generally much alike in character. Al-
together more than twenty different
zonal soils (often called Great Soil
Zones) have been recognized over the
earth. Of the soil formation factors
listed previously, the amount of rainfall, conditions of temperature and other climatic factors, and the length of
time are the most important in the development of the Great Soil Zones.

Where rainfall is heavy and temperatures are warm the minerals in the
soil that are needed for plant growth
are rapidly dissolved or leached out.
These soils are high in iron compounds
which rust and leave a reddish color.
Under such conditions the dead leaves
and roots decay rapidly and leave little
organic matter in the soil. Many of the
finer clay particles are carried from
the A horizon and deposited in the B
horizon. The A horizon may become
coarse in texture and poor in quality.

49

Where rainfall is heavy and temperatures are cool, leaching of minerals will be rapid. In such areas iron compounds are also leached leaving the lighter colored silica. Leaf decay under such conditions will be slow so that often a thick mat of leaves or pine needles will accumulate. Acids that develop in the leaf mat may cause the leached soils underneath to become acid in reaction. Such soils are usually poor in quality.

In areas where rainfall is light and temperatures moderate there will be less leaching of the soils. Under less rainfall, grasses will replace the forest vegetation. Leaf and grass decay will be moderate, thus heavy to moderate amounts of organic matter will accumulate in the soils, often giving them a dark color. Some of the best soils of the world develop in grassland areas. Kansas lies mostly in the grasslands province and has developed some of the world's finest soils.

Of the more than twenty Great Soil Zones of the world, nine of these are recognized in Kansas (Plate C). Three of these soils are found almost exclusively in the eastern half of the state. These are the Prairie-Forest, Prairie, and Reddish Prairie. The Black (Chernozem) soils occur in both the eastern and western halves of Kansas. The other five zonal soils, found in western Kansas, are the Chestnut, Dark Reddish Chestnut, Light Reddish Chestnut, and Gray (Semidesert) soils.

Prairie-Forest soils are developed under a tall, grass-deciduous, hardwood forest type vegetation. Rainfall is moderately heavy and leaching has removed some of the plant food minerals. In places claypans have accumulated in the subsoil so that certain areas are limited for agricultural use. It is usually

Caterpillar Tractor Company

Preparing Land for Cultivation. A tractor equipped with No. 6S Bulldozer is leveling an old drainage ditch in preparing land for cultivation on the Roy Leroy farm near Great Bend, Kansas.

50

necessary to apply lime and fertilizer to the Prairie-Forest soils, but under good management most of them will give some of the highest yields obtained anywhere in Kansas. Because of the favorable climate these soils often produce higher yields than the better soils farther west. A wide variety of crops may be grown on the Prairie-Forest soils. Usually corn, oats, and hay crops for the livestock industry are the most profitable.

Prairie soils are generally considered the most productive soils in the United States. They are almost as fertile as the Black (Chernozem) soils and are found in areas with a more favorable climate. Prairie soils develop under a tall grass vegetation and only a small amount of leaching occurs. Much organic matter and nitrogen have accumulated in these soils, allowing high crop yields. Corn, wheat, oats, and hay are the main crops. The wheat and some of the corn are sold for cash, but most of the crops support a livestock economy based on meat animals, dairy products, and poultry.

Reddish-Prairie soils are located in southern Kansas toward the south-central border. These soils are developed under higher temperatures than the Prairie soils and where the iron content is higher. They are usually more reddish in color. The native vegetation is tall and short prairie grasses. Rainfall is less plentiful and only a small amount of leaching has occurred. These are excellent soils. The principal crop is wheat, but considerable amounts of hay and sorghums are raised to support a growing livestock industry.

Black (Chernozem) soils are located in north-central Kansas. These are perhaps the best soils in Kansas. The limited amount of rainfall and high evaporation limit the kind of crops that may be planted, often causing a marked yield reduction or even a crop failure. The limited rainfall is enough to dissolve the calcium salts but is not enough to leach out the salts. As a result there is generally a calcium carbonate (lime) accumulation layer about eighteen to thirty inches below the surface. A mixed tall and short grass vegetation cover adds to the organic matter accumulation and gives the soils a deep black color. Black soils lie in the heart of the Kansas wheat belt. Sorghums are the second most important crop and considerable corn is grown along the northern border.

Chestnut soils have developed on the High Plains of western and northwestern Kansas. These soils formed under an average annual rainfall of fifteen to twenty inches and where evaporation is high. The natural vegetation on the Chestnut soils is short grass. As a result the amount of organic accumulation is less than in the Black soils, thus Chestnut soils are not quite so fertile. Color of the soils is lighter, ranging from a chestnut-brown surface layer to a light brown subsurface with a white calcareous (lime) accumulation at a depth of sixteen to twenty-four inches below the surface. The parent material is mostly a silty loess. Drought often causes a reduced crop yield and sometimes a crop failure. Wheat is the major crop of this area. Corn is fairly important in the north, but farther south, where the moisture supply is more uncertain, sorghums for grain and forage are widely grown. In

Caterpillar Tractor Company

Modern Soil Conservation. A tractor equipped with No. 6S Bulldozer and Hyster winch is removing trees from farm land on a farm near Great Bend, Kansas.

places where surface or ground water is available, considerable irrigation is practiced with resulting high yields. Dry-farming is practiced over much of the Chestnut soils area. *Dry-farming* is a method whereby a portion of the land is plowed but left fallow (unplanted). The land is cultivated occasionally to kill the weeds and to keep the soil loose enough to hold the rain water or melted snow. The second year this land is planted to wheat or sorghums. Dry-farming allows two years of rainfall for growing one crop.

Dark Reddish Chestnut soils developed on the mixed grass and short grass plains over parts of the Great Bend Prairie and the Red Hills. They are similar to the Chestnut soils but were developed under warmer temperatures. The reddish parent rock allows a dark reddish-brown upper surface over a light brown to light red subsoil. The parent material is a tough shale. A heavy grass cover contributes organic matter and a darker color in the A horizon. Winter wheat and sorghums are the principal crops. Some hay crops are grown in the eastern part and dry-farming is practiced in the western.

Light Reddish Chestnut soils differ from the Dark Reddish Chestnut because in a drier climate the short grass is more widely spaced and contributes less organic matter to the A horizon. The parent material consists of sands and other lighter materials. The principal crops are winter wheat and sorghums. Considerable dry-farming is practiced. The soil is generally less fertile than the Dark Reddish Chestnut.

Brown soils have developed in extreme western Kansas. They exist under a semiarid climate and a native vegetation of short grasses, bunch grasses, and shrubs. The surface soils are brown and the subsoils, at depths ranging from twelve to twenty-four inches, grade into a light gray or white calcareous (lime) layer. The drier the climate the closer the calcareous layer is to the surface. This area lies in the "dust bowl." Farming is uncertain and wind erosion is sometimes severe. Extensive dry-farming is practiced with wheat and grain sorghums as the principal crops. Brown soils are somewhat lower in organic material and nitrogen because of the sparse vegetation, but high enough in fertility to give good yields during years of favorable rainfall.

Gray (Semiarid) soils are located along the Arkansas River next to the western border of Kansas. These soils are sandy and are not generally usable for farming. The soil horizons are poorly developed and the soils are generally infertile. The area is used mostly for rough grazing of range livestock.

Soil Destruction

The early settlers of Kansas, as well as many of the later farmers, did not understand how to use the soils of the state. They applied methods that were old, or methods that would work only in areas of greater rainfall. The farmers planted crops that took much food from the soil. Crop rows were plowed up and down the slopes. Pastures and meadow lands were burned over. The soil, no longer protected by nature's cover of vegetation, was then moved by the rains and winds. Inch by inch the topsoil began to slip away. Seldom did the farmer realize that erosion was robbing him of his richest soil.

Sheet erosion, the moving of the topsoil a little at a time, has increased each year. As roots, leaves, and other organic matter have been removed, the run-off of water after each rainfall has become greater; thus, erosion has become greater. Unproductive subsoils that had for many centuries been covered with fertile topsoil are now at the surface. Gradually the farmer began to realize that his soil was being washed away.

Department of Agronomy, Kansas State University
Gully and Sheet Erosion in Jefferson County in Eastern Kansas

Wind Erosion in Seward County, Western Kansas

Gullies are the result of incorrect methods of farming. Water, pouring out of the furrows that have been plowed up and down the slope, carries much soil with it. As the sponge-like topsoil is removed by sheet erosion, gullies become longer and more numerous. Fields that once produced large crops have become so cut up that they can no longer be farmed and some have had to be abandoned. Thousands of acres in Kansas that produced good crops when first plowed by the early settlers are now useless for crop production.

The burning of fields destroys protective covering. It also destroys some of the necessary organic matter in the ground. The ability of soil to absorb water is reduced. Burning aids erosion by making it easier for wind and water to carry away the soil.

Floods result when fields are stripped of their topsoil and are cut by deep gullies. Soil, unprotected by the binding grass roots and trees, robbed of its organic matter by burning, and tilled in rows that run up and down slopes, loses its power to hold the rainfall. Rushing water can bring destruction to a farm that has been abused. Hundreds of acres of rich bottom land have been damaged by flood waters. Crops have been washed out. Unproductive subsoil from hillsides has been deposited over fertile soil. In 1951 the Kansas River not only flooded many hundreds of farms, but also caused much destruction in the towns and cities near it.

Wind erosion and dust storms are also the result of poor farming methods. In the dry areas, especially in the High Plains, when the earth is left uncovered, strong winds have moved much of the topsoil far away. In some places great sand dunes, as along the Cimarron and Arkansas rivers, have formed and now cover land that once was valuable.

54

The soils of Kansas have been greatly misused. The modern farmer is adjusting his uses of land to fit his natural surroundings. More and more he is using the latest and best methods of soil conservation.

Soil Conservation

Most farmers and ranchers of Kansas have learned that if they are to stay in business they must practice conservation. President Taft defined conservation as "the greatest good, for the greatest number, for the longest period of time." *Conservation*, then, is the use of the soil, or grass, or water, or mineral, or whatever the item may be, to its best advantage, for the greatest number of people possible, for as long as possible. Kansas soils and other natural resources have not been used this way. Much Kansas soil has been lost by erosion (Table 5). Kan-

sas farmers were not the only ones ruining their soil. The farmers in all of the states were doing the same thing.

TABLE 5
SOIL EROSION IN KANSAS

METHOD OF EROSION	ACRES ERODED
Wind erosion, destroyed . .	411,000 acres
Wind erosion, severely eroded	5,386,000 acres
Sheet erosion	7,628,000 acres
Severely gullied	3,475,000 acres
Land area of Kansas outside cities	52,520,949 acres

The people of the United States realize now that the future of the country depends upon the farmers and ranchers. In 1935 Congress passed an act creating the Soil Conservation Service.

To take advantage of this act, the people in an area vote to form a soil conservation district. The Soil Conservation Service will then send trained

Modern Soil Conservation in Practice. Soil conservation service is important in the life of Kansas. The scene shows a field with terrace slopes being farmed on the contour and grass waterways to dispose of excessive surface water. It is located in Brown County about one mile east of Reserve.

Department of Agronomy, Kansas State University

Flint Hills Located in Manhattan. This is a good example of uses of range land in the Flint Hills in Riley County. The scene shows an overgrazed pasture to the right of the fence and a well-managed pasture to the left.

men into the district to aid the farmers. The men will test the soil to see what needs to be added to make it productive again. They will suggest the kind of crops that should be planted, and they will help the farmer plan ways to prevent the various kinds of erosion. The Soil Conservation Service makes machines of various types available to the farmer at very low cost.

Soil conservation is the proper care and use of the land. It means using the land to produce the greatest amount of things most needed, and at the same time protecting the soil so that it will not lose its fertility. Each field or acre must be used for the things for which it is best suited and must be protected according to its needs. All measures that help keep the soil productive are tools of conservation. Terraces, contours, addition of organic matter, cover crops, grass, fertilizers, crop rotation, drainage, and irrigation are conservation tools. Soil conservation includes any and all methods that will aid the land in production without damaging it. To show how this can be done experiment stations have been established in various parts of the state.

Soil conservation does much more than safeguard the land. It increases crop yield, thus lowering the cost of production. It helps check drought damage to crops, pastures, and meadows. It reduces the amount of sand and silt washed into streams and lakes. It helps prevent floods by holding the water on and in the soil instead of letting it run off rapidly. Farmers who practice conservation estimate that it has increased their yields by at least 30 per cent.

Ranchers also need to practice conservation, even though the lands are never plowed. Where the pastures are

GREAT SOIL ZONES

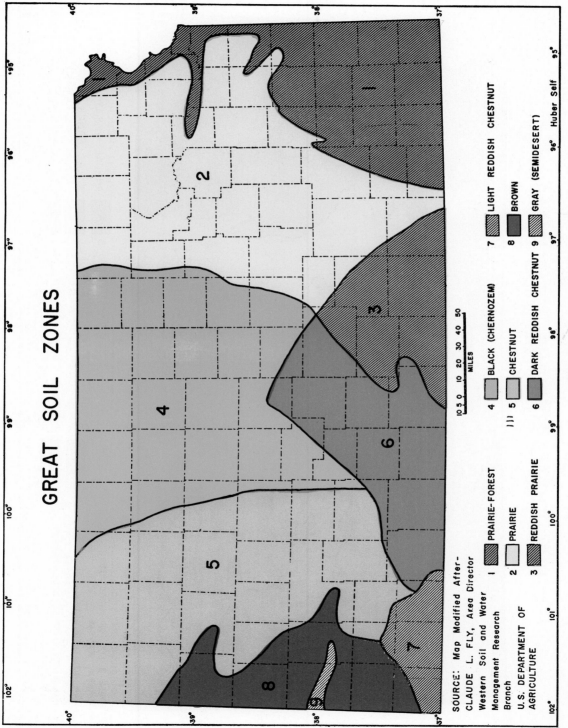

SOURCE: Map Modified After-
CLAUDE L. FLY, Area Director
Western Soil and Water
Management Research
Branch

U.S. DEPARTMENT OF
AGRICULTURE

1 PRAIRIE-FOREST
2 PRAIRIE
3 REDDISH PRAIRIE

4 BLACK (CHERNOZEM)
5 CHESTNUT
6 DARK REDDISH CHESTNUT

7 LIGHT REDDISH CHESTNUT
8 BROWN
9 GRAY (SEMIDESERT)

MILES
10 5 0   10 20 30 40 50

Huber Self

Plate C

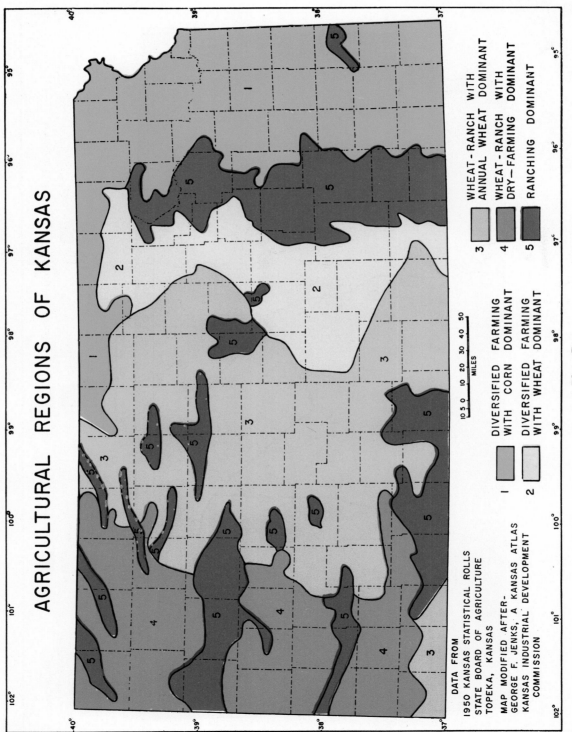

AGRICULTURAL REGIONS OF KANSAS

DATA FROM
1950 KANSAS STATISTICAL ROLLS
STATE BOARD OF AGRICULTURE
TOPEKA, KANSAS

MAP MODIFIED AFTER-
GEORGE F. JENKS, A KANSAS ATLAS
KANSAS INDUSTRIAL DEVELOPMENT
COMMISSION

10 5 0 10 20 30 40 50
MILES

1 — DIVERSIFIED FARMING WITH CORN DOMINANT

2 — DIVERSIFIED FARMING WITH WHEAT DOMINANT

3 — WHEAT-RANCH WITH ANNUAL WHEAT DOMINANT

4 — WHEAT-RANCH WITH DRY-FARMING DOMINANT

5 — RANCHING DOMINANT

Plate D

overgrazed, the best grasses are killed. The new grass replacing the old grass is often coarse and will not add as much weight to the animals. Ponds must be built where they will catch the most water, and pond spillways built for proper drainage. Weeds and brush must be mowed and good grasses planted.

Of all the problems facing ranchers, the greatest one is the prevention of grass fires. Carelessness in throwing lighted matches, cigars, and cigarettes out of car windows into grass along the highway is the cause of many fires which spread to the pastures and destroy hundreds of acres of good grass. Many ranchers attempt to control fires by grading a strip about twelve feet wide along each fence. This makes a wide path of bare ground over which the fire cannot pass unless there is a strong wind.

STUDENT ACTIVITIES

1. Visit a road-cut near your home. Try to locate the different soil horizons. Examine them carefully and note the differences.

2. What is soil conservation? Why should all farmers practice soil conservation? Do the farmers in your community practice soil conservation?

3. How is soil formed? Why is soil important to human health?

4. On an outline map of Kansas draw in the large soil divisions. Mark your home on the map. What kind of soil do you have in your community?

5. List ways in which man has destroyed the soil. In what ways can people living in towns and cities help protect the soil?

6. Which part of Kansas has the greatest amount of soil erosion? Why?

7. What do the following words mean?
   a. residual soil   e. humus
   b. transported soil   f. organic matter
   c. alluvial   g. parent rock
   d. loess   h. calcareous

8. Why is dry-farming not practiced in eastern Kansas?

9. What is the relationship between soil formation and vegetation?

10. Make a soil profile by putting the different kinds of rocks and soils in the correct order in a glass fruit jar. Explain to the class why they appear in the order they do.

11. Ask the county agent to talk with your class about soil conservation in your community. What does he think the farmers need to do to conserve soil? How can you help conserve soil?

12. How many pupils in your class live on farms or ranches? What conservation methods are used on their home places? Why?

Chapter 7

THE PEOPLE OF KANSAS

The progress and importance of a country or state depends largely upon three basic factors. These factors are the size and kind of territory, the resources of the area, and the type of people. A country or state can be too small to become great. It may be too cold or too unhealthful. The little country of Luxembourg, between France and Germany, has only 999 square miles. It is smaller than any one of fifteen counties in Kansas. Luxembourg can never hope to be a great country as long as it remains so small. Also an area must have resources for people to use if it is to make progress. Some of the states west of Kansas have very few people. Little has been found in them for people to use. Finally the type of people in a place determine what will be done about the opportunities found there. Some people seem to be fitted for doing some things, but not others. In China the people have succeeded in producing large quantities of foods from their small farms, yet they have done little in developing manufacturing, mining, and commerce. Before the discovery of America by the Europeans the American Indian had done little. At the time the white people were developing the eastern and southwestern part of the United States, the Indians of Kansas were ignoring most

Manhattan Mercury Newspaper

A Street Parade in Manhattan. The population of Kansas is varied. People of all ages and with **many** interests live in our state.

opportunities. They were contented with hunting, fishing, and very crude agriculture.

It is fortunate that Kansas, as is true of our country in general, finally was occupied by an advanced and energetic people. The hardy pioneers who entered Kansas in the Great Westward Movement had already proved themselves. In this new territory these pioneers followed examples set since Jamestown and Plymouth. Descendants of these and others who entered the state make up much of the 2,000,000 population of Kansas today.

The Settlement of Kansas

The settlement of Kansas started a long time before white people came into the area. Scattered Indian tribes of unknown numbers lived in what is now Kansas. Most of them moved from place to place as they followed the buffalo. These Indians had no horses, cattle, or sheep. Their only domestic animal was the dog. Many lived in tepees made of hides. A few, like the Wichita Indians, lived in grass-covered homes.

The first white people to travel in Kansas were the Spanish explorers led by Coronado. These men came to Kansas in 1541. This was sixty-six years before the settlement of Jamestown and seventy-nine years before the Pilgrims landed on Plymouth Rock. Although the Spanish did not make any permanent settlements, a few did stay and live with the Indians. Later other Spanish leaders also guided expeditions across the territory. The Spanish traders from Santa Fe were the only whites coming into the area until after 1700. During this time the Indians acquired horses from the Spanish.

The French explorers of North America claimed for France all the land drained by the Mississippi River. This claim included all of what is now Kansas. After 1700 many Frenchmen visited the area. Most of them came to trade with the Indians or to explore. The first attempt at white settlement in what is now Kansas was about 1795 when a group of French farmers moved from Missouri Territory to what is now Doniphan County. After two years, however, they returned to their old homes.

In 1803 when the United States purchased Louisiana Territory, all of what is now Kansas except the southwestern corner became a part of the nation. This southwestern area was added when Texas joined the United States and adjusted its boundaries. Soon after the Louisiana Purchase white people moved into the eastern part of the state to secure farms, build homes, and trade with the Indians.

After the purchase of Louisiana the government of the United States sent many people to explore the vast territory. Among those visiting Kansas were Lewis and Clark, who explored along the Missouri River. Pike traveled from east to west across the state. In 1821 trade was started between the Kansas City area and Santa Fe, then a city in the country of Mexico. This trade followed the route that became known as the Santa Fe Trail, and passed through or near the present cities of Council Grove, Great Bend, Dodge City, and Garden City. Also, the Oregon Trail, over which passed the thousands of persons moving to or

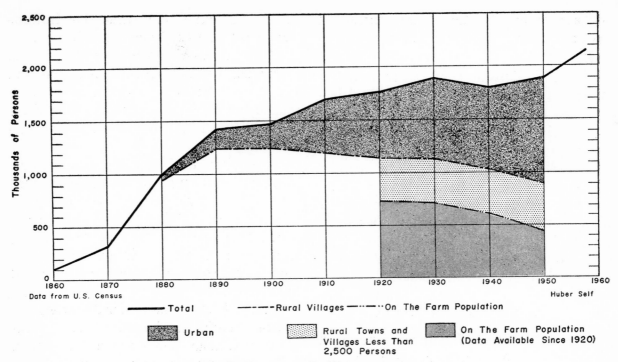

Huber Self

——— Total   — · — Rural Villages — · · — On The Farm Population

Urban   Rural Towns and Villages Less Than 2,500 Persons   On The Farm Population (Data Available Since 1920)

Population Growth in Kansas 1860-1958

toward the west coast, crossed northern and eastern Kansas.

As settlement in the Louisiana Territory increased, new states were formed and added to the Union. A large area was soon organized as Kansas Territory. By 1860 the territory had been reduced in size and shape to the present state of Kansas. In 1861 Kansas became the thirty-fourth state in the United States. By this date many white people had settled in the area. Also the nation was at the beginning of the Civil War. A large majority of Kansans were opposed to slavery and the state remained loyal to the Union. This did not prevent fighting within the state, however, and history records many bloody encounters between the Kansans and the raiders from southern territory.

Kansas gained a large portion of its population between the years 1860 and 1890. This rapid gain was due mainly

to improved farm machinery, cheap land, and promotional activity of the railroads. Settlers came from the older areas in the United States and many immigrants came from Germany, England, Sweden, Russia, and other European countries. The greatest percentage increase was from 1860 to 1870 but the greatest absolute increase was from 1870 to 1880, when there was a gain of 631,679 persons, making a total of 996,096 in 1880. Most eastern Kansas counties had their greatest increase in population before 1900 but many of these counties have experienced a gradual decline since 1900. Most western counties have experienced their greatest gain in population since 1900.

Between 1890 and 1930 the population of Kansas increased steadily, but at a much slower rate. During the ten-year period from 1930 to 1940 there was a slight loss in population as people moved from the western part of the state. Since 1940, however, the population of Kansas has been increasing again.

As the Plains Indians were moved from Kansas to reservations in Oklahoma, white settlement spread westward. The first whites to use much of western Kansas were the cattlemen. Soon they were challenged by the farmers. These early farmers often lived in dugouts or sod shanties. Windmills and barbed-wire fence usually marked a homesite. Soon they were plowing the land and growing large crops of wheat and other grains. Since these early days many minerals have been found, irrigated projects started, manufacturing developed, and some small villages have expanded into great cities.

Kansas Population Today

Every ten years the government of the United States takes a census. This census is a listing of the people living in every community and rural area. It gives the age of each person, where each was born, his or her nationality, the kind of work each does, and other important information. The census reports tell the number of people in each community, village, town, or city, each county, and each state. By comparing the reports for each ten-year period, one can determine which places have gained in population and which have lost. In Kansas the population is also enumerated each year by the county assessors and these figures are used by the Kansas State Board of Agriculture in its reports.

In 1950 the official United States census of Kansas indicated 1,905,299 persons were living in the state. The 1958 population of Kansas, as esti-

mated by the Kansas State Board of Agriculture, was 2,100,665, or a gain of 194,366 since 1950. The population of Kansas went above the 2,000,000 total for the first time in 1955. In 1956 Kansas had 52.6 per cent of its population classed as urban and 47.4 per cent classed as rural. The urban classification includes all cities having a population of 2,500 or more persons. All towns and villages having fewer than 2,500 persons and all people living in the country are classed as rural. On the farm, population has decreased rapidly since 1920. Of the total population of Kansas, 41.6 per cent lived on the farm in 1920, 37.5 per cent in 1930, 33.6 per cent in 1940, and only 23.3 per cent in 1950.

The population of Kansas is unevenly distributed over the state, ranging from large cities such as Wichita and Kansas City to rural areas having an average of less than one person per square mile. Naturally not all parts of the state are equally attractive for making a living. In general, more people live in the better, more pleasant, and more attractive places. Most people will live where they can make a good living.

The population gain or loss per county between 1951 and 1956 is shown on Map 10. During this five-year period a severe drought caused farm incomes to decline. As a result many people moved from the farms to cities within the state or migrated to other parts of the nation. So great was the movement that fifty-nine of the 105 counties of Kansas lost population. In spite of this loss, however, the state as a whole gained a total of 158,605 persons between 1951 and 1958.

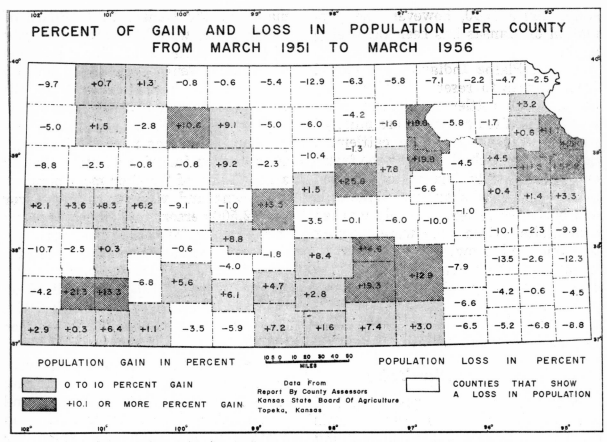

Map 10. Per Cent of Gain and Loss in Population Per County, March 1951-1956

The principal factor in population growth within the state is the change from an agricultural economy to a balanced economy between agriculture and manufacturing. Mineral production also gives work to many people. The major sources of income for the people of Kansas, in the order of their importance, are manufacturing payrolls, trade and service payrolls, farm income, construction, and mining payrolls.

Forty-six counties had population increases between 1951 and 1956. The counties having the greatest percentage increases were Johnson with 58.2, Saline with 25.8, and Grant with 21.3. Geary, Riley, and Sedgwick counties all had population gains of between 19 and 20 per cent. The counties having the largest actual gain were Sedgwick and Wyandotte. Located in these two counties are the state's two largest cities— Wichita and Kansas City.

Population increases in the various counties may be the result of several factors or only one activity. For example, the population growth of Riley, Geary, Dickson, and Saline counties can largely be accounted for by the expansion of the Fort Riley and Schilling (Smoky Hill) military bases. Many people moved into Sedgwick County because of the great industrial expansion. The gain in the southwestern corner of the state in such counties as Grant, Stevens, and Haskell is due largely to the expansion of the Hugoton Gas Field.

Active petroleum development in Pawnee, Barton, Ellis, and nearby counties caused many people to move into that area. Also, expanding irrigation farming has likely caused population increases in Ford, Greeley, Scott, and many other western counties.

Fifty-nine of the 105 counties had population losses during the period from 1951 to 1956. Six of these counties, however, lost less than 1 per cent of their population. Seven counties lost 10 per cent or more. Of these seven, four (Bourbon, Chase, Coffey, Woodson) are in the eastern, two (Jewell, Lincoln) are in the central, and one (Hamilton) is in the western part of the state (Map 10). Woodson had the greatest percentage loss, 13.5 per cent.

Bourbon and Cherokee had the greatest actual losses. The population of each decreased about 2,000 persons. In general, population losses in the eastern part of the state were caused by the declining production of coal, lead, and zinc. Losses in the western part of the state are due largely to declining agricultural production.

Map 11 shows the distribution of population in Kansas. Each dot on the map represents 1,000 persons. The closer the dots are together the greater the number of people living in the area. In the larger cities and towns the dots make a continuous black pattern. Wichita and Kansas City, the two largest cities, had populations of over 250,000 and 131,000, respectively, in 1958. The

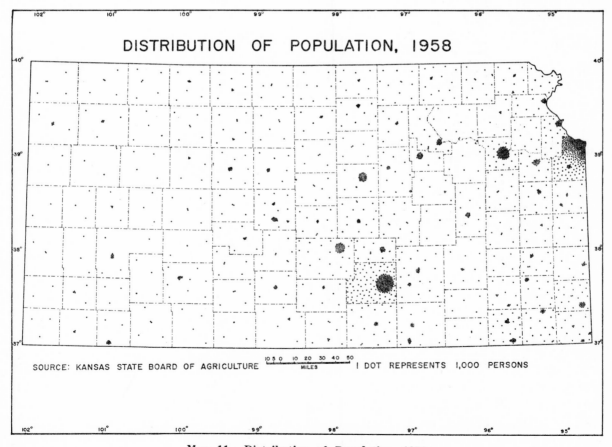

DISTRIBUTION OF POPULATION, 1958

SOURCE: KANSAS STATE BOARD OF AGRICULTURE   MILES   I DOT REPRESENTS 1,000 PERSONS

Map 11. Distribution of Population, 1958

EMPLOYMENT PAYROLLS IN KANSAS, 1957

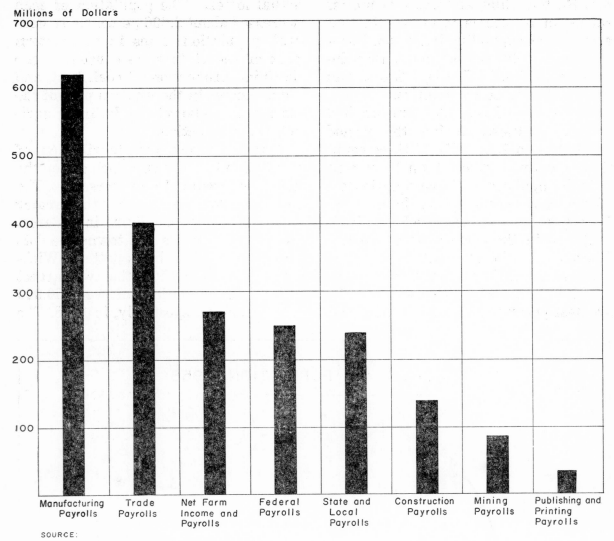

Millions of Dollars

SOURCE:
KANSAS INDUSTRIAL DEVELOPMENT COMMISSION
TOPEKA, KANSAS

state capital, Topeka, has over 110,000 persons, and Hutchinson, Salina, Lawrence, and Leavenworth each has a population of over 20,000. Four of the largest cities—Kansas City, Topeka, Lawrence, Leavenworth—are either in or border the Glaciated Region. Wichita and Hutchinson are in the Great Bend Prairie, and Salina is in the Smoky Hills Region. All of these cities, along with sixteen others that have populations between 10,000 and 20,000, are located in the eastern half of the state. Only five cities—Dodge City, Garden City, Great Bend, Hays, Liberal—in western Kansas have more than 10,000 persons living in them. The largest of these is Great Bend that has a population of 17,184.

The most densely populated rural areas are also in eastern Kansas. Because the people are classed as rural does not necessarily mean that they live or work on farms. The large rural population in the Ozark Plateau, Cherokee Plain, and Osage Cuestas regions is largely accounted for by the large number of small mining communities in the coal or zinc areas. Fertile agricultural lands in the Glaciated Region and the Great Bend Prairie are very productive and, therefore, support many rural people.

Large wheat farms and ranches require much space for their activities, but do not require many people to carry out those activities. The Flint Hills, High Plains, Smoky Hills, and Red Hills regions are areas of fewer people because of their activities. The two counties having the smallest populations are Stanton and Greeley. Both are located along the Colorado border in the drier part of the High Plains.

In 1950, Kansas had 1,790,384 persons listed in the census as native-born white Americans. The number of foreign-born white people is not large, approximately 38,577. Some of these people were born in Canada, England, Ireland, France, Union of South Africa, Australia, Germany, or other countries. The Negro population of Kansas, in 1950, was 73,158. Many people now listing Kansas as their home were born in other states of the United States. Many native-born Kansans, however, have moved to other states.

Kansas has a comparatively young population. The average age of all males in the state is 30.6 years and the average age of the females is 31.5 years.

This means that a large proportion of the people are available for the development of the state, and that additional numbers will soon be finishing school to take their place in the business world.

STUDENT ACTIVITIES

1. Is your county more or less densely populated than the state average? Why?

2. Is your county gaining or losing population? Why?

3. Why is the western part of the state not as densely populated as the eastern part?

4. Which natural regions have the greatest population density? Why? In what ways are they alike?

5. What is the relationship between population density and rainfall? What maps can you use to prove your statement?

6. On a map of Kansas locate the five largest cities. Are they in regions of large or small population density?

7. Has the rural population of Kansas increased or decreased? Why? Has the urban population increased or decreased? Why?

8. Which five counties of Kansas have the largest population? Which five have the greatest population per square mile?

9. In which state were your parents born? Where were your grandparents born? How many of your classmates were born in Kansas? Were any of your classmates born in another country?

10. How does Wichita compare in size with St. Louis? Oklahoma City? Omaha? Denver? Des Moines?

Chapter 8

AGRICULTURE

Agriculture is the basic occupation of Kansas and the world. Areas that have favorable combinations of land surface, climate, soil, and good location for the efficient production of important crops or livestock are among the most fortunate geographically. Agriculture employs 21 per cent of the working population of Kansas. This is not quite so many as are engaged in wholesale and retail trade or in service occupations. However, the production of food and raw materials from the soil, natural vegetation, minerals, and other resources must be present before the trade and service occupations can exist. The annual value of crops produced in Kansas is somewhat less than the cash value of minerals. Still, agriculture employs eight times as many as the oil fields and mines, and utilizes much more of the state's land.

Agriculture had a leading part in the economic development and history of Kansas. Pioneer families a hundred years ago raised most of their own supplies, but had only a few products to sell. As railroads moved westward across the state between 1865 and 1900, the agricultural area also expanded. Most of the state's income then came from wheat farming or livestock ranching. Since 1900, cities have grown large. Oil, coal, and other minerals, as well as manufacturing, now compete with the farms as producers of wealth. Agriculture has continued to expand, however, and new crops and livestock products have become important. Today, Kansas farmers can no longer

Kansas State University Agricultural Extension

Irrigation in Western Kansas. In many irrigation areas water is put on the field by siphoning it from the main ditch to rows between the crops in the field.

66

Field of Grain Sorghum. Grain sorghums are an important farm crop in Kansas. This scene shows a moisture and nitrogen study being made of grain sorghum at the Fort Hays Experimental Station.

make great expansion into new areas, but much can be done to improve and increase production in most of the farming areas now being cultivated.

Kansas agriculture is on a large scale. In 1954 there were 120,140 farms and ranches with an average area of 438.2 acres. They occupied a total of 50,023,538 acres, which is 95.2 per cent of the land area of the state. Approximately 29,577,170 acres are ready for the plow and 21,440,232 produce crops in an average year. More than a hundred different crops and livestock produce an average cash income of over $950,000,000 per year.

Factors in Agricultural Production

Knowledge of the geographic environment is more important in agricul-ture than in any other enterprise. Man can do relatively little to improve the relief of the land, climatic conditions, or a physical condition of the soil in areas so large as those required for field crops and pasture. A favorable combination of surface, climate, soil, and other factors together in one place are necessary to make a productive farming area. However, not all of these are usually found under favorable conditions in the same place. Where some of these conditions are good it may be possible to improve the others. Areas of good soil and favorable surface may be irrigated. Easily cultivated but infertile soils in a mild climate may be fertilized. It is usually necessary to fence the land and clear away native vegetation before crops can be grown.

Plains are the most common land

form in Kansas. This favors the use of agricultural machinery. Fields can be large. Soils were originally deeper on plains. In such locations soils are less rapidly eroded than if the surface were more steeply sloping.

A moderately long and warm growing season with an abundance of sunshine favors plant growth in most parts of Kansas. Over much of the state winters are mild enough for animals to graze on the range. In some parts of the state it is possible for pastures to grow all winter. In the areas of lower elevation, in eastern Kansas, oats, corn, potatoes, soybeans, grapes, apple seedlings, truck, and feed crops can be grown. In much of the western parts of Kansas, drought-resistant crops must be planted due to the decrease in rainfall. Some of the drier and rougher parts are best suited for range livestock.

Types of Farming Areas

Kansas crops and livestock are highly varied. Even those that are raised in most parts of the state are much more important in some areas than in others. Although many farms and ranches give their chief attention to one product, they usually have other production at least for home use. No two farms or ranches are exactly alike. However, farmers living close together are likely to be dealing with similar climate, soil, natural vegetation, and other conditions. Thus, it often happens that their farms are a great deal alike. They find it profitable to operate in about the same way. The sameness gives the basis for types of farming areas. On Plate D the type-farming areas have been grouped into five large divisions based upon the principal items produced.

Department of Horticulture, Kansas State University

Commercial Vegetable Production. The sprinkler irrigation system is used to maintain ideal moisture conditions for watermelons and sweet corn on Britts Farm on the Kansas River near Manhattan, Kansas.

68

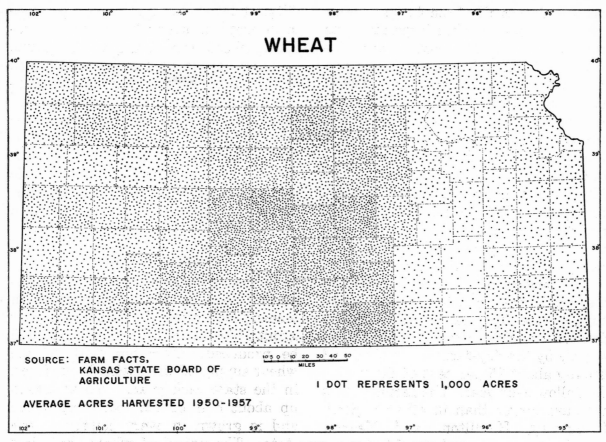

WHEAT

SOURCE: FARM FACTS,
KANSAS STATE BOARD OF
AGRICULTURE

AVERAGE ACRES HARVESTED 1950-1957

1 DOT REPRESENTS 1,000 ACRES

Map 12. Average Acres of Wheat Harvested 1950-1957

Eastern and northeastern Kansas is a region of diversified agriculture in which corn is the chief crop (Map 14). This area has much in common with the adjacent areas in Missouri and Nebraska. Livestock—beef cattle, dairy cattle, hogs, poultry—is fed much of the corn and from the sale of these animals most of the farm income is received. In addition to corn, such crops as hay, wheat, oats, and soybeans are also raised. Most farms will raise three to five different crops in addition to the livestock kept. Extending across the region in the valley of the Kaw River is an area of very productive land. This valley is farmed intensively and produces good crops of vegetables, hay, and corn.

The western part of the Flint Hills and the area just west of it form a region of diversified agriculture in which wheat is the chief crop. In this region the farms vary in size from 200 to 500 acres. Most farms produce **a variety** of crops including oats, **grain sorghums, alfalfa, and soybeans. Dairy** cattle, especially near the larger cities, and sheep in Sedgwick County are important sources of income. Beef cattle are to be found on most farms.

Much of the west central part of Kansas is dominated by a wheat-ranch type of agriculture (Plate D, area 3). In this region wheat is the important crop, so controlling the area that the only other crop of great value is grain sorghum. Although beef cattle are

69

kept on almost all of the farms, the income from wheat is much greater than that received from livestock and livestock products. Seldom do farms produce more than two crops and most of the income from livestock is from the sale of beef cattle. The principal area for the raising of grain sorghums is Morton, Stevens, and Seward counties, but production has been increasing rapidly in all western counties in the last few years. In this part of the state practically all the land is put into production each year. Wheat may be raised in the same field for many years.

The western part of the High Plains also has a wheat-ranch type of agriculture (Plate D, area 4). Wheat production in this region, however, is largely by the dry-farming method and usually about 15 per cent of the region lies fallow each year. The farms in this area are larger than in other regions. In Greeley, Hamilton, and Kearny counties, they averaged over 1,700 acres each. At various places in this region, as well as in the west central part of the state, irrigation projects have been developed. Irrigated areas near Scott City, Syracuse, Garden City, Dodge City, Larned, and Kinsley produce such crops as sugar beets, melons, alfalfa, wheat, corn, and grain sorghum.

Large areas of pasture and ranch lands are to be found throughout Kansas (Plate D, area 5). They are more numerous in the western than in the eastern half of the state. It must be noted, however, that the largest continuous area is in the Flint Hills. Cattle are by far the most important animals, although sheep are numerous in certain areas.

Leading Field Crops

Wheat is the leading crop in Kansas and Kansas is the leading state in wheat production. In an average year about 186,000,000 bushels of wheat will be produced. Over one fifth of the wheat supply of the nation is produced in the state each year. Wheat makes up about half of the total crop value and is grown in every county of the state. The principal wheat-producing area, however, is the western two thirds of the state, with central Kansas the largest producing area.

In general, wheat farms are large, varying in size from 400 to over 1,000

TABLE 6
PRINCIPAL FIELD CROPS, 1956

CROP	PRODUCTION	ACRES HARVESTED	FARM VALUE
Wheat	143,282,000 bu.	9,244,000	$286,564,000
Corn	32,067,000 bu.	1,527,000	44,894,000
Sorghum (grain)	24,390,000 bu.	1,626,000	30,488,000
Oats	23,177,000 bu.	1,078,000	17,151,000
Barley	10,404,000 bu.	578,000	9,780,000
Soybeans	3,018,000 bu.	355,000	6,388,000
Hay (all kinds)	2,433,000 tons	2,275,000	62,042,000
Sorghum (silage)	2,961,000 tons	658,000	31,090,000

Harvesting Wheat in Early Summer. Kansas wheat is usually ready for cutting in early summer. Large fields and level lands make the use of machines easy and profitable. Frequently many machines work in the same fields at the same time.

acres in size. Since the production of wheat requires less labor than many of the farm crops, and most of the work is done by machines, the farmers have added to the size of their farms. Wheat belongs to the grass family. It grows best on prairie lands like those of the Great Bend Prairie, Wellington Plain, and the Smoky Hills regions, where the land is fairly level and the rainfall is between twenty and thirty inches a year. The High Plains are also important producers of wheat. The principal kind of wheat planted in Kansas is winter wheat. Winter wheat is planted in the fall. It grows slowly during the winter, more rapidly during the spring, and is harvested the following summer. The state is a part of the Hard Winter Wheat Belt of the United States.

For the most part, farm life functions around the planting and harvesting of the wheat crop. Ground for the crop is plowed in the late summer or early fall so that farmers may take advantage of the summer and fall rains. It is harrowed to prepare a good seed bed. The seed is then planted in rows by a drill. If the soil is warm and moist, the seed will sprout and green blades appear above the ground in a week or two. The young wheat grows rapidly and soon the fields look like big yards of grass. By the time of the first frost, the wheat may be several inches high.

Having the wheat growing like this is good soil conservation. The roots of the wheat hold the soil in place and prevent it from blowing. Most wheat farmers usually keep several head of beef cattle or sheep. The wheat serves as good pasture for the stock during the winter. In some places shelter belts have been planted to aid soil conservation. A shelter belt is formed by rows of trees planted to prevent the wind from blowing directly across the field.

With the coming of spring the wheat starts to grow rapidly. Cattle are taken from the fields. During May the heads begin to form. By June the wheat stock and heads turn yellow, then brown, as they ripen. When the wheat is ripe it is the harvest season. This is the busiest time of the year in the wheat belt.

Wheat in the southern part of the state ripens first. Crews of men with trucks and combines move from place to place harvesting the crops. The combine is a large machine that moves itself through the fields of wheat. Large blades, which are a part of the machine, cut off the heads that contain the grains of wheat. The heads are caught on a belt and carried up into the machine where the seeds are separated from the rest of the head. The seeds are then either carried through a hose into a truck moving beside the combine, or are stored in a tank carried on the combine. The tank, when filled, is emptied into a truck.

After the wheat is threshed, it is taken to an elevator where it is stored until shipped to market. During the harvest season trucks often form lines one-half mile to a mile in length waiting to get to the elevator. Even small towns in the wheat area will have one or more elevators. Often an elevator is built in the open country, beside a railroad, where there is no town. During the

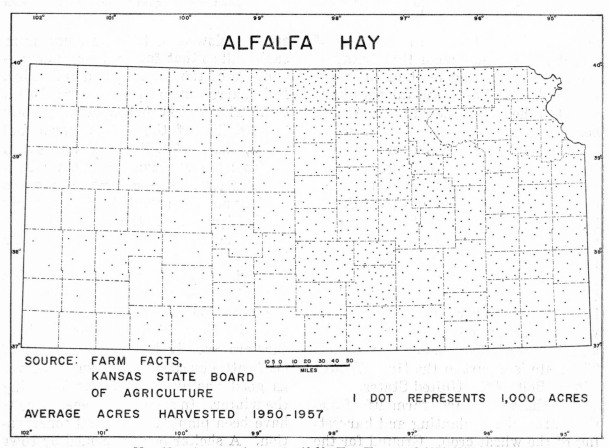

Map 13. Average Acres of Alfalfa Hay Harvested 1950-1957

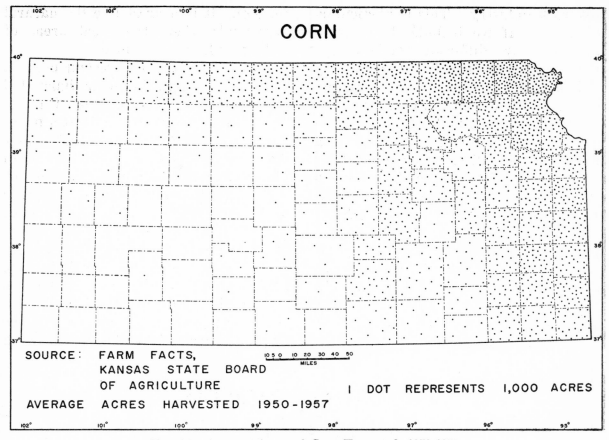

CORN

SOURCE: FARM FACTS,
KANSAS STATE BOARD
OF AGRICULTURE
AVERAGE ACRES HARVESTED 1950-1957

MILES

1 DOT REPRESENTS 1,000 ACRES

Map 14. Average Acres of Corn Harvested, 1950-1957

harvest season the railroads move many extra trains of boxcars into the wheat country to carry the grain to market.

Kansas wheat is shipped all over the world. As trains leave the elevators, they may go to flour mills located in Wichita, Hutchinson, Kansas City, or other places within the state. There are many small as well as large flour mills within Kansas. Much wheat is sent to St. Louis and Chicago. Some is shipped to Houston and other seaports to be transhipped to Europe or Asia.

Hay is second in acreage and also second in value among Kansas crops. The approximately 2,300,000 acres of hay harvested amount to about 25 per cent of the harvested acreage of wheat.

The crop of 1956 was valued at about $62,000,000, but in some years it has exceeded $80,000,000. During the ten-year period 1945-1954 Kansas ranked fourteenth among the states in hay production. Like wheat it is grown in all counties of the state.

The distribution of the hay crop varies considerably, both in acreage and in the different varieties. In Kansas the principal tame hay crops are alfalfa, lespedeza, clover, and timothy. Of these, alfalfa is by far the most important, accounting for almost 75 per cent of the total value of the yearly hay crop. The distribution in varieties of hay shows direct relation to soils.

The hay crop is used in many ways. It is more essential than corn in the livestock industry. This is particularly obvious if we include the grazing provided by different varieties of hay. For more than half the year the animals live primarily by grazing. Through the winter, however, hay may provide the great bulk of feed. Even hogs depend far more on grazing than many people realize. The extended use of hay for silage is adding importance to the crop. In recent years hay, notably alfalfa, is being dehydrated (dried), ground, and used as bagged feeds, either in pure form or mixed with grain. Hay also fits well into the average farm program. Besides the feeding value, it is an important crop in rotation and soil conservation. A grass cover provides the best protection for soil. It is nearest like the natural grasslands where the great areas of richest soils were formed.

Corn is usually the second crop in value but fourth in acres harvested among the major crops of Kansas. Three facts about corn make it a popular crop. First, corn is easily produced. The Indians and American pioneers grew corn with the crudest of tools. On the other extreme, corn is one of the easily produced crops with the most modern machinery. Second, more uses have been found for it than for any other crop. These include home preparations for the table, numerous commercial products, and the most common ingredient in livestock feeds. Third, in areas favorable for growing

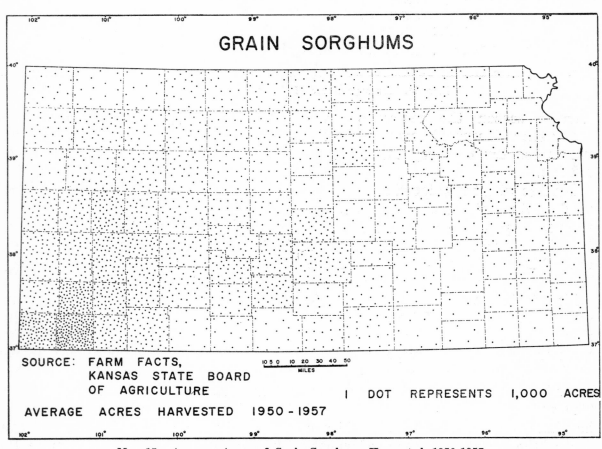

GRAIN SORGHUMS

SOURCE: FARM FACTS,
KANSAS STATE BOARD
OF AGRICULTURE
AVERAGE ACRES HARVESTED 1950-1957

1 DOT REPRESENTS 1,000 ACRES

Map 15. Average Acres of Grain Sorghums Harvested, 1950-1957

74

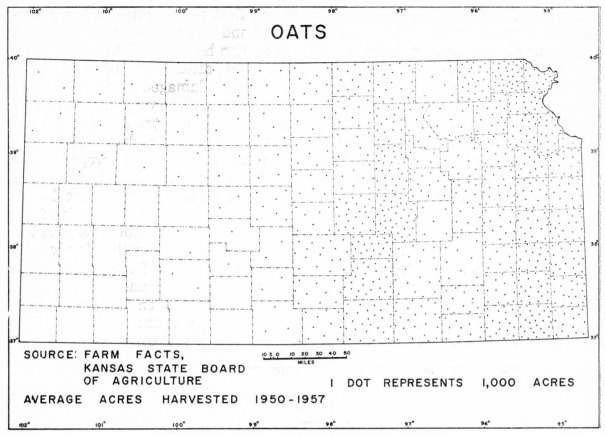

OATS

SOURCE: FARM FACTS,
KANSAS STATE BOARD
OF AGRICULTURE

AVERAGE ACRES HARVESTED 1950-1957

I DOT REPRESENTS 1,000 ACRES

Map 16. Average Acres of Oats Harvested, 1950-1957

corn, it produces the greatest number of bushels and the most food value per acre of all the grain crops.

Much attention has been given to the improvement of corn. This has been done in three ways—by selecting the choice ears year after year, by crossing different types, and by producing hybrid seed. The first method has been used throughout most of our history. Later, different types of corn were crossed. More recently the different process of producing hybrid corn has been developed. Each method has been important, but the production of hybrid corn has been most significant. It is claimed that this type of corn will increase production about 20 per cent. Still further gains have been made by soil improvement. In the last quarter century corn production per acre has been increased about 33 per cent.

Although some corn is grown in each county in Kansas, most of the production is confined to the Glaciated Region, the Osage Cuestas, the Cherokee Plain, and the northern part of the Smoky Hills Region (Map 14). Over 88 per cent of the total corn crop is produced in the eastern third of the state. In the Glaciated Region corn grows especially well on the rich alluvial, glacial, and loessal soils, and the land is level enough to be easily cultivated. However, most of the region is rolling, and the frequent tillage required for corn may result in much erosion. Most of the corn grown in Kansas is fed to the

75

livestock in the state. Corn production averages around 35,000,000 bushels per year and has an average farm value of approximately $46,000,000 annually.

Sorghums produced in Kansas are used for three things—grain, forage, and silage. Grain sorghums rank second in acreage but fourth in value among the major crops (Table 6). The yield is almost 25,000,000 bushels annually which have a farm value of over $30,000,000. In some years the value of sorghum produced for silage exceeds that of grain sorghum. Sorghums are grown in all parts of the state, but the chief producing area for grain sorghum is the southwestern part of the High Plains. Finney, Grant, Morton, Stevens, and Seward counties all rank in the first ten counties in acres harvested and bushels produced. Sorghum production has expanded rapidly in recent years, often replacing corn that is more easily damaged by drought.

Sorghums have very extensive root systems that penetrate deep into the soils. They are more drought resistant than other important crops. Grain sorghums are grown in cultivated rows much like corn. Where there is danger of wind erosion only the heads of the grain are cut and a tall stubble is left to protect the soil until it is planting time again. Most of the production is sold as a cash crop and the remainder is fed to livestock on the farms.

Oats occupy about 1,400,000 acres, chiefly in the eastern third of Kansas

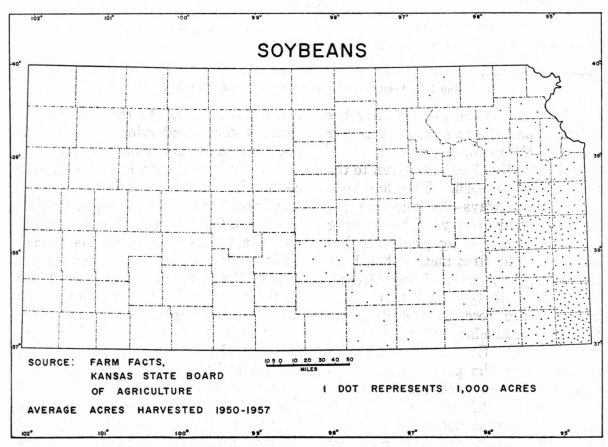

Map 17. Average Acres of Soybeans Harvested, 1950-1957

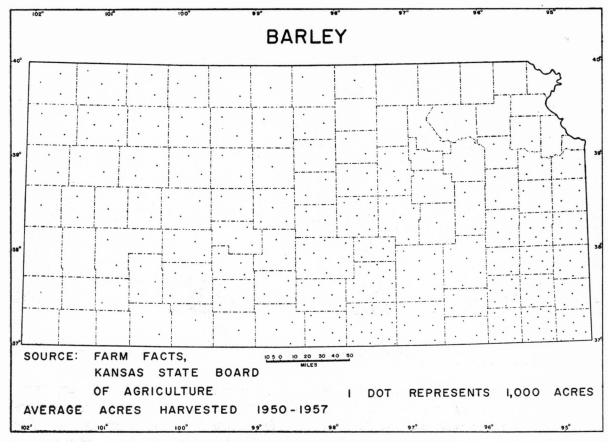

BARLEY

SOURCE: FARM FACTS,
KANSAS STATE BOARD
OF AGRICULTURE

AVERAGE ACRES HARVESTED 1950-1957

MILES

I DOT REPRESENTS 1,000 ACRES

Map 18. Average Acres of Barley Harvested, 1950-1957

(Map 16). This crop occupies more acreage than any other crop except wheat in the southeastern part of the state. Some counties in the far western part of the state produce only small amounts of oats if any at all. Most of the oats are sown in the early spring and are harvested in June or July. They may be pastured or cut as a grain crop.

Rye, barley, flax, broomcorn, cowpeas, and soybeans are among the lesser crops grown by Kansas farmers. Of these crops, barley and soybeans are by far the most important. In an average year over 350,000 acres will be planted in soybeans and over 800,000 acres in barley. The chief area for the production of each is in the eastern part of the state. In most years the value of the barley crop exceeds $10,000,000 and the value of the soybeans $3,000,000.

Truck, Vegetable, and Fruit Crops

Truck and vegetable crops of one kind or another are grown in most parts of the state. Probably vegetable gardening is the most common agricultural production in Kansas. Great numbers of the town and city population carry on gardening regularly. So many vegetables can be grown on very small plots that gardening is practical in the crowded spaces of urban people. Home gardening is favorable in many ways.

The Kaw River Valley is an area of

77

Harvesting Beets. This scene around Garden City shows the beets being harvested by a mechanical digger. The beets are carried to the truck and the tops and waste material put back on the ground. It is plowed into the soil and helps fertilize it.

intensive cultivation. Here the land is planted in such crops as potatoes, corn, beans, and peas as well as alfalfa and wheat. The income per acre in this valley is great because of the large production, but it also costs more per acre to farm the land so intensively. The Kaw Valley extends from Manhattan

INCREASE IN IRRIGATION ACREAGE IN KANSAS 1890-1958

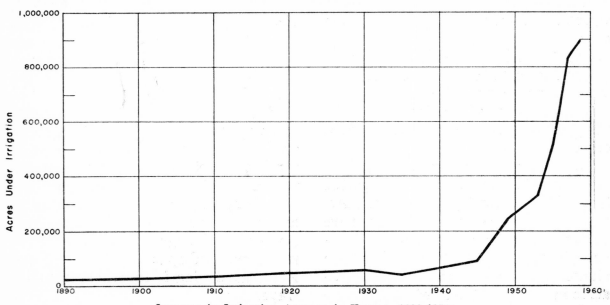

Increase in Irrigation Acreage in Kansas, 1890-1958

78

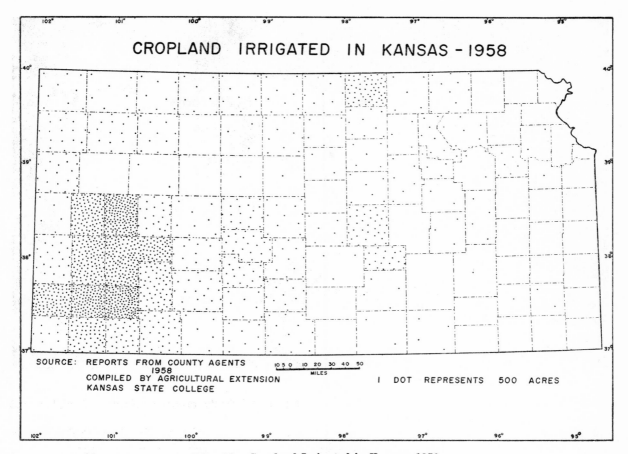

CROPLAND IRRIGATED IN KANSAS - 1958

SOURCE: REPORTS FROM COUNTY AGENTS
1958
COMPILED BY AGRICULTURAL EXTENSION
KANSAS STATE COLLEGE

MILES

I DOT REPRESENTS 500 ACRES

Map 19. Cropland Irrigated in Kansas, 1958

eastward to Kansas City, and is one of the most densely populated parts of the state, making it an important market for vegetables and potatoes. These products are not only used by the people in the area, but they have an outlet in northern and eastern markets.

Irrigation has been highly developed in many areas in the western part of the state. Along the Arkansas River in the vicinity of Garden City, Dodge City, and Larned, water is taken from the river, or from large lakes formed by dams across the river, to irrigate a variety of crops. Near Meade water for irrigation is supplied by artesian wells. In other places wells have been drilled into the ground water and the water pumped to the surface. Among the various irrigated crops are grain sorghum, wheat, sugar beets, alfalfa, melons, and vegetables, especially onions and beans. Although these crops do not occupy large acreages, they are of special importance to the area in which they are produced. All the commercial production of sugar beets and onions is in the western irrigated areas. In an average year the onion crop will have a value of over $600,000 and sugar beets will exceed $1,400,000 in value. Such farming is always intensive (Map 19).

Apples and strawberries are the two principal fruit crops in terms of value, but neither is as widely grown as

79

Baskets of Apples. Apples and strawberries are the principal fruits grown in Kansas. Doniphan and Reno counties are the leading producers of apples.

peaches or grapes. The production of commercial apples is confined to thirteen counties in the eastern half of the state. Doniphan County ranks first, Reno County second in both the number of bushels and the value of the apples produced. In 1956 peaches were produced in all Kansas counties except Morton. The two counties leading in production were Wyandotte and Sedgwick and the chief area for production was the Glaciated Region. During the past few years strawberry production has been greatly increased. The 1956 crop amounted to 648,000 pounds, an increase of 44 per cent over 1955.

STUDENT ACTIVITIES

1. Select some purpose for which corn is used and report on the processes involved in preparing it for that use.

2. Ask a local farm implement dealer for pictures for display purposes. Explain the use of each machine.

3. Where are the principal wheat-producing areas of Kansas? Why are they located there? What is the relationship of these areas to landforms and climate?

4. Compare the crop maps with the map of natural regions. Which region leads in production of wheat? Corn? Sugar beets? Grain sorghums?

5. What are the chief agricultural products of your county? What uses are made of these crops?

6. Plan a field trip to a farm. Make a list of questions you want to ask the farmer as well as a list of things you want to see and do.

7. Prepare a quiz program on "Agriculture in Kansas."

8. Compare the crop map with the soil map. In what ways are these maps alike? In what ways do they differ?

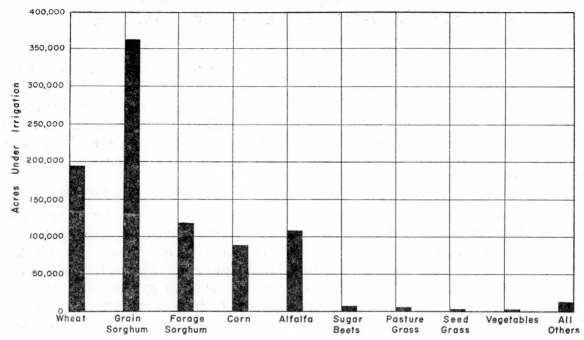

1958
ACRES OF MAJOR CROPS UNDER IRRIGATION IN KANSAS

9. Why is little corn grown in the southwestern part of the state and little wheat in the southeastern part?

10. Make a list of as many uses for wheat as you can. How have you used wheat today?

11. What does each of the following terms mean?
   a. dry-farming   d. rotation of crops
   b. irrigation   e. combine
   c. cash crop

12. Write a paper comparing life on a wheat farm with life on a truck farm.

Chapter 9

LIVESTOCK AND LIVESTOCK PRODUCTS

Livestock-raising is big business in Kansas and is growing rapidly. The value of cattle alone is now double the pre-World War II figure. Livestock and livestock products make up about 53.1 per cent of the entire cash income from Kansas farms. Kansas markets large numbers of hogs, cattle, and calves yearly. Dairy products and poultry and eggs, despite large home consumption, also add greatly to the annual cash income of the state's farmers. The number of sheep in the state is much smaller than the number of cattle, although in certain areas sheep-raising is among the major livestock enterprises. Practically all sheep and lambs, as well as wool, are sold. Cash receipts from marketings of livestock and livestock products amount to over $467,000,000 yearly. The position of Kansas as a producer of livestock is aided by favorable climate much of the year, rich grasslands, and breeders who are trying to produce even finer breeds for the farms and ranches.

The Grass Resources

The grasslands of Kansas are among the state's greatest resources. They originally covered over 75 per cent of the land area. The best soils developed under cover of grasses and were protected from erosion by them. The early development of Kansas was based largely on the range cattle industry. Pastures still provide about half of the feed for the livestock population.

Kansas Industrial Development Commission

A Herd of Hereford Cattle. The Hereford is one of the most common types of beef cattle pastured on the ranches of Kansas.

An Aerial View of the McKinley-Winter Livestock Commission Company. Cattle buying and selling is still big business in Dodge City. This aerial view shows the livestock pens, sales auditorium, and loading chutes for railroad stock cars that can be placed alongside the pens.

The grasslands of the state differ greatly. The Flint Hills have a luxuriant bluestem that is high in feed value. The Osage Cuestas and the Glaciated regions, and some of the more humid areas, have tall, nutritious grasses. Much of central Kansas has a mixture of tall and short grasses. Short grasses prevail in the High Plains. Many species of grasses and wildflowers compose the grasslands. Some of the most widespread of the native grasses are big and little bluestem, side oats grama, blue grama, and buffalo. Bermuda, Johnson, carpet, and dallis grasses and several kinds of clover and lespedeza are among the pasture plants that have been purposely or accidentally introduced. Some of them have spread to all parts of the state. Bermuda and Johnson grass are excellent for livestock, but are a nuisance in cultivated fields.

The grassland resources of Kansas have been as badly abused as the soils. Large areas have been destroyed to make way for crops. In many cases this was unwise and soil erosion followed. Almost all the range lands have been overgrazed. Some of the Kansas

83

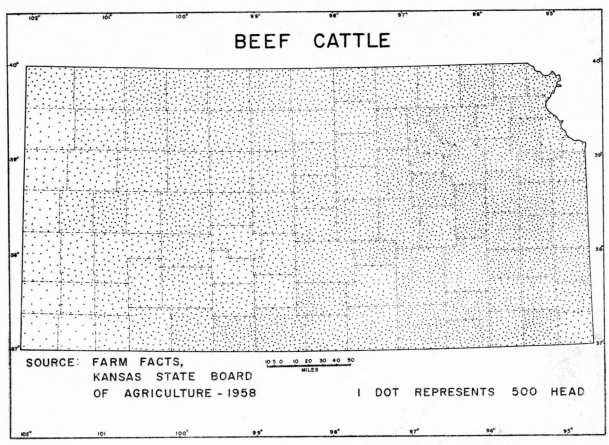

BEEF CATTLE

SOURCE: FARM FACTS,
KANSAS STATE BOARD
OF AGRICULTURE - 1958

10 5 0 10 20 30 40 50
MILES

I DOT REPRESENTS 500 HEAD

Map 20. Beef Cattle in Kansas

grasslands, like those along the bottoms of the Smoky Hills River in Dickinson County, can safely provide forage for one cow for every two acres, while the Flint Hills require four to eight acres for one cow. Some parts of the High Plains, however, require twenty-five or more acres for each animal. Overgrazing causes a decline in carrying capacity. Undesirable plants replace those preferred by livestock. Some of these may be poisonous.

The grasslands of Kansas now have only about 50 per cent of their original grazing capacity. Many areas are now incapable of supporting the number of livestock that they once did. Some of the range lands, however, recover quickly when given proper man-

agement. In other cases more costly improvement measures are necessary. Special care is required to maintain the plant cover in the more arid areas where nature's balance is easily upset and hard to restore. Kansas farmers and ranchers are now working with agricultural experts to improve the grazing lands of the state.

Cattle

Cattle and calves in Kansas number approximately 4,200,000 head. Of these, 508,000 are milk cows, and some of the calves are replacements for the dairy herds. Most are eventually used for beef. About 3,000,000 are intended chiefly for beef production. The value of cattle and calves amounts to about

84

$341,000,000. This is 89 per cent of the total value of all livestock.

Beef cattle have been important in the history and economy of Kansas for a long time. Even before the Civil War cattle were being driven from Texas through the eastern part of the state to Missouri. With the coming of the railroads the cattle industry flourished. Cattle towns such as Abilene, Ellsworth, Newton, Wichita, Caldwell, Hunnewell, and Dodge City became famous as shipping centers. The railroad would build to the town. Soon large cattle pens were built and many new businesses started. Cattle from Texas and the Indian Territory were then driven to the center for shipment to eastern markets. As the railroads extended their lines west many of the eastern towns decreased in population and importance since the western cities were closer to where the large herds entered Kansas. In 1871 over 700,000 head of cattle were driven to Abilene by almost 3,000 cowboys. By 1873

Wichita had become the chief shipping center when 405,000 were moved eastward from that city. By 1883, however, the principal shipping center had again shifted westward, Dodge City receiving and shipping over 350,000 head.

In the early 1870's stock-raising in central Kansas was becoming important. Many of the cattle driven into the state from the south had a disease called Texas fever. Later some coming into Kansas were found to have the hoof and mouth disease. Because of these diseases the Kansas legislature, in 1885, passed a law that prohibited the driving of Texas cattle into or through Kansas between March 1 and December 1 of each year. At about the same time farmers began to settle on the western grazing lands. They plowed the fields and put up barbed-wire fences. By 1890 the great cattle drives had ended.

Beef cattle are now raised throughout Kansas. The greatest number per

Kansas State University

A Herd of Aberdeen-Angus Yearling Steers. A herd of Aberdeen-Angus yearling steers feeding on bluestem pasture in the Flint Hills.

The W. O. Boehle Herd in Lawrence, Kansas, 1957. The Holstein, Jersey, and Guernsey are popular dairy breeds in Kansas. The industry centers around the large cities and in areas favorable for the growth of grass for pasturage.

square mile are in the central and eastern part of the state (Map 20). The Flint Hills have more range beef cattle than any other region in Kansas. Butler County ranks first and Cowley County third among the counties of Kansas in the number of cattle and calves on farms. Both counties are in the Flint Hills. Lyon, Pottawatomie, Marion, Greenwood, Washington, and Wabaunsee counties, all partly in the Flint Hills, are also important producers of cattle. The good soils and mild, moist climate of the region produce more grass to the acre than any other part of the state. Hereford cattle are the most common animals found grazing in the Flint Hills, but Angus are also kept on many ranches and stock farms. In a few places the Brangus, a cross between the Angus and the Brahma, are popular. Most ranches and stock farms will have many head of feeder stock in addition to their regular beef cattle. Feeder stock is made up of animals purchased from the ranches of Texas, Wyoming, or some other state by the rancher. These ani-

mals graze on the rich grass and add many pounds of meat before being sold.

In the High Plains, Red Hills, Great Bend Prairie, and Smoky Hills regions are many large ranches. Barber County ranked fourth and Reno County tenth among the counties of Kansas in the number of cattle and calves. Many ranches in these regions have pure-bred stock, but the largest number of cattle are feeder stock.

The native buffalo grass of the High Plains is very nourishing. Since it is a dry-weather plant it can stand much heavy grazing. Because it is a short grass, however, its yield per acre is low, requiring about twelve or more acres for each animal unit. Most wheat farmers also graze many head of feeder stock. These animals graze on a pasture of winter wheat during the fall, winter, and early spring seasons. During the periods of heavy snows feed must be provided. The greatest handicap to the cattle industry on the High Plains is the severe blizzards. Frequently during these storm periods many hundreds of cattle freeze to death unless shelter can be found.

Beef cattle will probably become even more important in Kansas than they are now. With over forty meat-packing plants and many smaller slaughtering firms, Kansas ranks among the first ten states in the number of meat animals killed each year. In an average year the state accounts for almost 2,000,000,000 pounds of meat, most of which is beef. Progress in the beef cattle industry will include better breeds of livestock, improvement of range and pasture, and greater production of feed crops so that more cattle can be fattened for market in the state. This will enable the meat-packing industry to expand so that more of

the profit from the cattle business will enrich the Kansas people.

Dairy cattle also contribute much to the economy of the state. Dairy products in Kansas have an average annual farm value of over $75,000,000. It is obtained from approximately 443,000 head of dairy cattle. Many of the milk cows are Holstein, the animal which gives the greatest quantity of milk. Numerous dairy herds, however, are made up of Jersey cattle which are noted for the richness of their milk. Cows convert a large quantity of rough feeds and pasture into one of the best of all food products. Most dairymen have pastures and grow feed crops. Many of them purchase additional feed, particularly cottonseed meal,

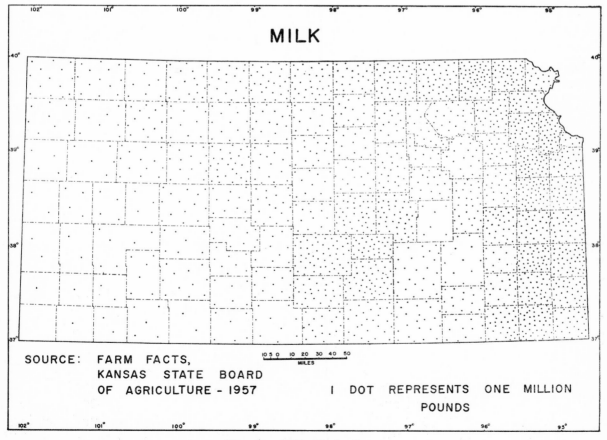

MILK

SOURCE: FARM FACTS,
KANSAS STATE BOARD
OF AGRICULTURE - 1957

I DOT REPRESENTS ONE MILLION POUNDS

Map 21. Milk Production

87

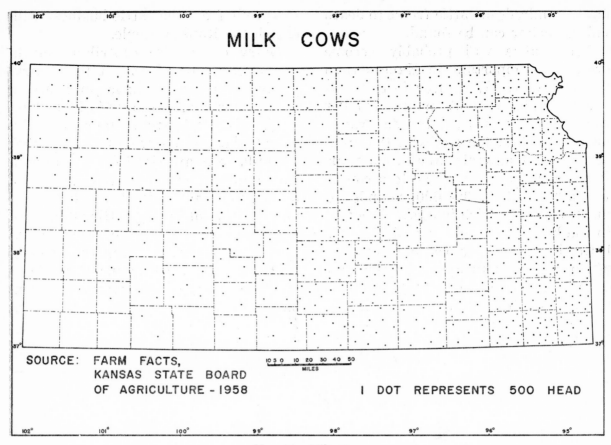

MILK COWS

SOURCE: FARM FACTS,
KANSAS STATE BOARD
OF AGRICULTURE - 1958

MILES

I DOT REPRESENTS 500 HEAD

Map 22. Milk Cows

wheat bran, and other factory by-products.

Kansas farms produce a large share of the state's fresh milk. The distribution of dairy cows is somewhat similar to that of people. There is a cluster of dairies near each of the larger cities. The principal dairy areas include the Great Bend Prairie, the Glaciated Region, the eastern part of the Osage Cuestas, and the Cherokee Plain.

In 1956 Kansas had forty-seven plants making butter, fifty-three making cheese, twenty-five producing condensed and evaporated milk, and eighty-seven that made ice cream. These industries are based on the production of almost 2,500,000,000 gallons of milk each year. Usually Kansas ranks tenth among the states in butter production which totals between 40,000,000 and 45,000,000 pounds annually. Cheese products amount to over 12,000,000 pounds, and ice cream production to almost 7,000,000 gallons yearly.

Sheep

Sheep in Kansas, in an average year, of approximately $7,500,000. Some number about 600,000 and have a value sheep and lambs are to be found in each county in the state, but the number per county may vary greatly from year to year (Map 23). The High Plains counties of Thomas, Hamilton, Finney, Stanton, and Meade are usually leaders in the number of sheep grazed. In this region the sheep feed on the winter wheat and grain sorghums during much of the fall and winter seasons. Often sheep are brought in from Colorado and Wyoming. Their grazing on the good Kansas pastures causes them to gain about ten pounds per month, or about sixty to seventy pounds during the grazing season. The sheep best suited to western Kansas have thick wool fleeces that protect them from the cold winter winds. Many farmers will have the sheep sheared in the spring before marketing them. In general, the average fleece will weigh about ten pounds.

In central and eastern Kansas the sheep are kept on smaller farms and usually in smaller numbers. Sedgwick, Dickinson, Harvey, and Reno counties are important producers. Except in Pottawatomie County not many sheep are raised in the Flint Hills. In the eastern and central counties most of the

sheep and lambs graze only in small pastures or are fed in feed lots. Some cities, such as Manhattan and Emporia, have large feed lots near the railroads where the sheep can be kept until they are ready to be shipped to market.

Very little wool is used by Kansas factories. Wool contains a great deal of grease and dirt. Washing it is a fairly complicated process that requires much pure soft water. This washing is not often done in Kansas. Most of the wool is shipped to factories in New England.

Swine

Hogs on the farms of Kansas number over 900,000 head in an average year and are valued at almost $15,000,000. The Glaciated Region is the principal swine-producing area with Nemaha, Doniphan, and Brown counties being the leaders (Map 24). Hogs are raised in all sections of the state, but

A Flock of Sheep. Sheep raising is common in many parts of Kansas. These animals are grown for both their wool and meat.

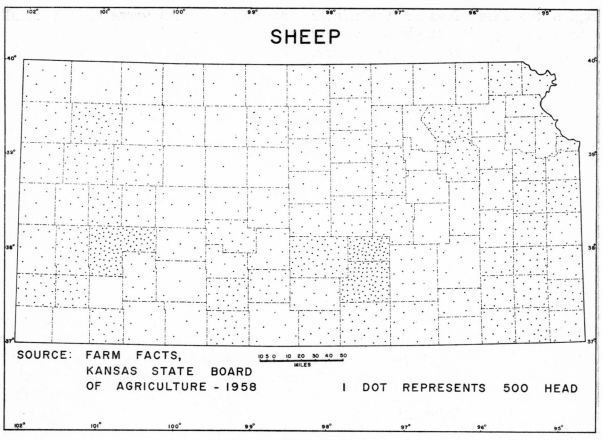

SHEEP

SOURCE: FARM FACTS,
KANSAS STATE BOARD
OF AGRICULTURE - 1958

1 DOT REPRESENTS 500 HEAD

MILES

Map 23. Sheep Production

in the High Plains they are fewer in number than either cattle or sheep.

Hog production has been important in Kansas since the time of settlement. In early times pork could be kept rather easily without refrigeration, and lard was in special demand for cooking. At that time vegetable oils and fats had not come into wide use. With the development of corn raising in Kansas, hog raising advanced as in the other corn-producing areas of the United States. Hog production and corn growing have always been closely related in the nation.

The distribution of hogs and corn in Kansas shows this corn-hog relationship (Maps 14 and 24). In the Glaciated Region where much corn is grown is also found a large percentage of the hogs. The High Plains, although it is much larger in area than the Glaciated Region, produces very little corn and only a small percentage of the hogs. The Osage Cuestas Region is the second most important hog-producing area. Most of the common breeds of swine are raised within the state. These include Poland China, Duroc, Hampshire, Berkshire, Yorkshire, and others. Interest in the improvement of breeds is similar to that of cattle.

Other Animal Industries

Horses and mules have been largely displaced by the use of tractors on farms. The number of horses and mules has dropped from 1,326,000 in

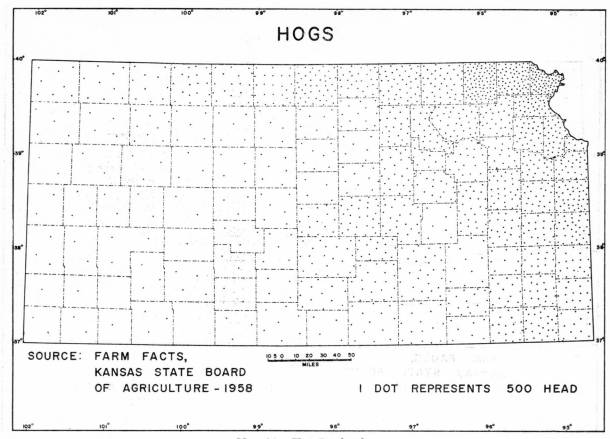

HOGS

SOURCE: FARM FACTS,
KANSAS STATE BOARD
OF AGRICULTURE - 1958

10 5 0 10 20 30 40 50
MILES

I DOT REPRESENTS 500 HEAD

Map 24. Hog Production

Department of Animal Hubandry, Kansas State University

A Herd of Hogs. Hogs are an important part of most corn-farm areas. The farmer makes **more money** by feeding the corn to the hogs and then selling the animals than by selling the corn itself.

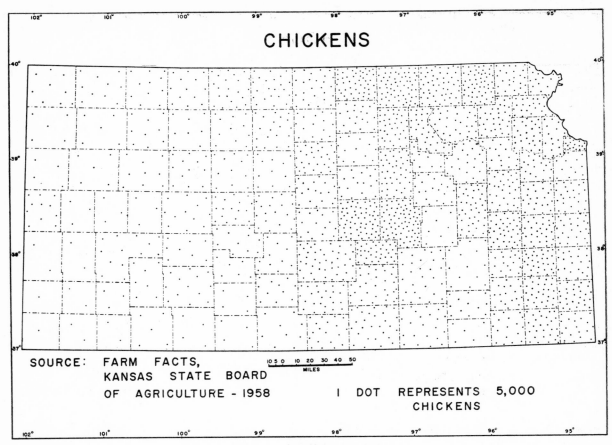

CHICKENS

SOURCE: FARM FACTS,
KANSAS STATE BOARD
OF AGRICULTURE - 1958   I DOT REPRESENTS 5,000
                                              CHICKENS

10 5 0   10 20   30 40   50
MILES

Map 25.   Chicken Production

Department of Poultry, Kansas State University

A Flock of White Plymouth Rock Chickens. A white Plymouth Rock poultry flock in Riley County, Kansas. A modern poultry house. Egg production is up to 70 per cent.

92

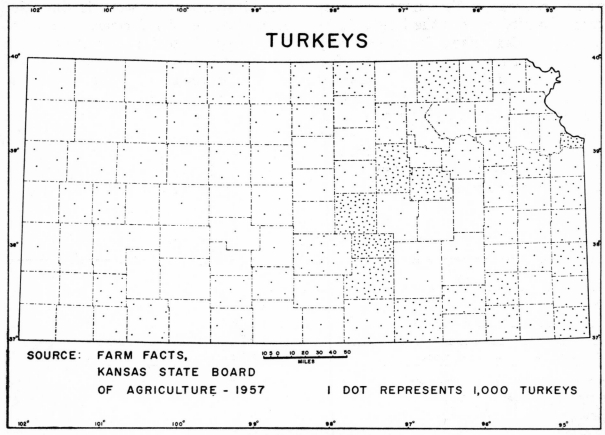

TURKEYS

SOURCE: FARM FACTS,
KANSAS STATE BOARD
OF AGRICULTURE - 1957   I DOT REPRESENTS 1,000 TURKEYS

Map 26. Turkey Production

1920 to 80,000 in 1956. Not more than half the farms of Kansas have either horses or mules, and about half the farms that keep these animals have only two each. Some farmers find it desirable to have one team to do certain work about the farm. The few mules are kept almost entirely for work animals. A large number of the horses are kept for riding. Many of these are owned by people who live in towns or cities.

Poultry production in Kansas is more widely distributed over the state than any other phase of livestock production. More than 120,000 farms and many inhabitants of towns and cities keep poultry in small numbers. The flocks vary in size from a dozen to several hundred. Chickens, turkeys, ducks, geese, and guineas are produced in large numbers, but chickens are by far more important than all the others combined. The total income from all poultry averages about $55,000,000 annually. That is over 5 per cent of all income from agriculture. Poultry and eggs make up almost 6 per cent of the cash farm income in Kansas.

Many people, both on farms and in urban centers, keep a few chickens to produce eggs and meat for home use. A few surplus eggs may be sold locally. On numerous farms are flocks of 100 to 400 chickens, kept for commercial egg production. In the past this has been the chief source of egg supply. The small flocks are more often fed with

93

grain produced on the farms or scraps from the kitchen, but the larger flocks likely are fed mixed feeds, carefully prepared for egg production. In a few cases the well-built houses are kept lighted all night, especially in the long winter nights, so the hens can get feed and water at any time. Still another plan in chicken production is that of the large producers who keep several thousand hens for egg production. In most instances this work is the chief occupation of the farmer. Many of these "egg factories" are near large markets where commercial ready-mixed feeds and markets for the eggs are handy. Many thousands of dozens of eggs are produced annually, from which is obtained well over half the total income from all poultry.

The broiler business has become quite important in recent years. In this type

TABLE 7
POULTRY INCOME AND NATIONAL RANK, 1956

ITEM	VALUE	NATIONAL RANK
Eggs sold and consumed	$42,775,000	17
Farm chickens, sales and home use	6,129,000	41
Broiler production	1,287,000	23
Turkeys, sales plus home consumption	3,871,000	38

Department of Poultry, Kansas State University

Part of a Flock of 4,500 Turkeys. William Lake Turkey Farm near Marysville, Kansas, in Marshall County. The tractor in the background drives over a few rows of corn each day and the turkeys feed freely from the downed and partially shelled ears of corn.

of production large, carefully arranged houses that hold from 3,000 to over 5,000 chickens each are prepared. One grower may operate five or more of these houses. Day-old chicks are purchased from commercial hatcheries. They are fed ready-mixed feeds from commercial mills. Feeding, watering, and temperature of the buildings are carefully regulated. In eight to twelve wee's the chickens are ready for market. By this method of production the quality of meat has been improved.

The turkeys raised in Kansas have numbered over 900,000 annually for several decades. However, production has shifted greatly from small flocks on many farms to large flocks on few farms. Some growers have flocks of 5,000 to 10,000 or more birds. They are allowed to grow all through the summer and sold in the fall, largely for the Thanksgiving and Christmas markets. The quality of turkey meat has been improved like that of the broiler chickens. The greatest area of production is in the eastern counties.

Ducks and geese are raised in moderate numbers for the market and for lesser extent for feathers. Guinea production in Kansas has declined during the past few years. A few people prefer guinea meat to that of chicken, but in general the sale is not great.

STUDENT ACTIVITIES

1. Explain why it can truly be said that "a dish of ice cream is pure grass."

2. In how many ways has grass served you today?

3. On a large map of Kansas locate the regions having the most cattle. The most sheep. The most swine.

4. Why are dairy cattle herds kept near large cities while beef herds are in the range country?

5. How could Kansans make more money out of their livestock industry?

6. Why is grass one of the most important resources of Kansas?

7. Which parts of Kansas have the largest ranches? Give reasons for their locations.

8. Why do wheat farmers often keep many head of cattle?

9. In which part of the state is the production of chickens and turkeys especially important? Why?

10. Make a collection of pictures of the different breeds of beef cattle and dairy cattle. In what ways do these animals differ?

11. What is the influence of topography and rainfall upon the livestock industry?

12. Why do different areas require different numbers of acres of land to feed one cow?

13. What is the relationship between the distribution of swine and the production of corn in Kansas? Why?

Chapter 10

MINERAL INDUSTRIES

It is often said that today people are living in a mineral world. Much that each individual uses daily is available only because of the minerals of the world. The family car, trains, buses, airplanes, and all other forms of transportation are all made in whole or in part from minerals. The kitchen stove, the furnace that heats the home in winter, the fan or air conditioner that cools the home in summer, the light bulbs, water fixtures, and even the springs of the beds are made from minerals. The engines that run the machines in factories and the machines used in the home are all made from minerals. Next to food and water, minerals are the most important items nature gives to man. Minerals are grouped into three large divisions—mineral fuels, metals, and nonmetals.

Mineral fuels, which include the useful items of coal, petroleum, and natural gas, were formed from organic substances. An *organic substance* is something that has life or did have life in the past. Coal has been formed from the remains of ancient plant life; petroleum and natural gas from the remains of ancient animal and plant life. Kansas is fortunate in that large deposits of all the mineral fuels are found in the state. Only the states of Texas, California, Louisiana, and Oklahoma produce more petroleum than Kansas; the state ranks fifth in the nation.

Metals and nonmetals are formed from *inorganic substances*. In other words, they are formed from things that do not and never have had life.

Kansas does not have many of the important metals: iron, copper, or uranium. Some lead and zinc are mined in the state and there are vast deposits of clay that contain much aluminum. The

TABLE 8

VALUE OF KANSAS MINERAL PRODUCTION

MINERAL	VALUE*
Crude petroleum	$351,500,000
Natural gas	58,000,000
Portland cement and masonry	29,000,000
Stone	25,500,000
Natural gas liquids	11,000,000
Clay and clay products	10,000,000
Salt	8,500,000
Sand and gravel	8,000,000
Zinc	5,000,000
Bituminous coal	4,000,000
Lead	2,600,000
Others	7,800,000

*1956 Estimate, Kansas State Geological Survey

state, however, does have vast quantities of nonmetallic minerals. The sale of salt and gypsum that are mined each year brings hundreds of thousands of dollars into the state. Gravel, sand, and stone are also important nonmetallic products of Kansas.

The great demand for minerals has been brought about by the material progress of man. In prehistoric times man made his tools from stone. Later man learned to fashion his tools from metals. The next step was making machines. This advance led man to develop machines that were powered by the use of other minerals. The chief minerals man has used to operate his machines are coal, oil, and gas. These

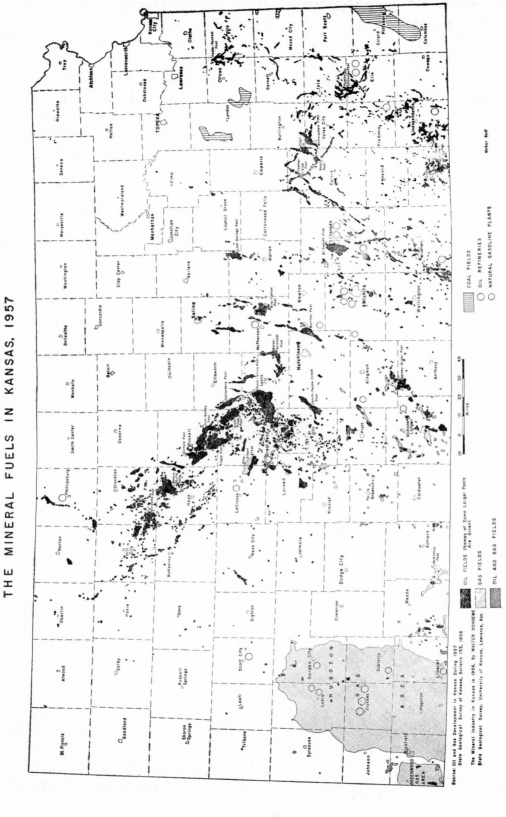

Map 27. The Mineral Fuels in Kansas, 1957

97

make up the mineral fuels which man must burn to produce the necessary energy to run his great machines. The American people have become the greatest users of minerals in the world.

Kansas ranks eighth among the states of the United States in the production of all minerals. Each year the production of minerals amounts to over $400,000,000. The state ranks high in the production of natural gas, petroleum, zinc, and salt. In all, twenty-one different minerals are mined each year, and there are five others that could be mined if necessary.

Mineral Fuels

Petroleum is the most important mineral product mined in Kansas. Its total value is much greater than the total value of all other minerals combined. Petroleum and natural gas are produced in seventy-nine counties (Map 27). The principal areas of petroleum production are in the central and southeastern parts of the state. In the southwestern part of the state, especially in the counties of Stevens, Grant, Kearny, Finney, Haskell, and Seward, is located the Hugoton Natural Gas Field, the largest in the United States.

Where many oil wells are found close together, they form an oil pool. Fields may be either large or small. No two pools will have the same shape or the same number of wells. The largest of the Kansas oil pools are the Silica-Chase in Stafford, Barton, and Rice counties; El Dorado in Butler County; Trapp in Russell and Barton counties; Kraft-Prusa in Ellsworth and Barton counties; Bemis-Stutts in Ellis and Rooks counties; and Hall-Gurney in

Russell and Barton counties. All the oil pools in Kansas form a part of the great Mid-Continent Oil Field of the United States.

Oil in Kansas was first developed in the eastern part of the state. In the early 1880's over 100 wells were drilled near Paola, but none had much oil, since ten barrels a day was the amount given by the best producer. Since that early date, the oil-producing area has extended southward and then westward. The greatest oil-producing year for the state was 1956 when 124,476,-713 barrels were brought to the surface. Since 1950, oil production in Kansas has increased gradually from approximately 100,000,000 barrels per year to over 124,000,000. At present there are approximately 41,650 producing wells in the state.

The petroleum used today was formed hundreds of thousands of years ago. It is thought to be the remains of plant and animal matter that has undergone great changes. These changes were caused by heat and pressure as the lands were being folded, broken, or forced from one position to another. As the rocks were being changed, the oil accumulated in places known as *structural traps*. An *anticline*, which is an upfolding of rocks, is the most common type of structural trap in Kansas. The shale layer above the oil and gas is so solid that the liquid cannot get through. Petroleum is found in rock that is porous. In Kansas, sandstone is the principal type of rock in which oil is found. Oil is found above water because it is lighter than water and will float on it. Gas is at the top because it is lighter than either.

Drilling methods are of two types,

rotary and cable tool. The rotary method is the most modern and is used in Kansas. It is safer, cheaper, and faster for drilling deep wells in formations that are soft and may cave in, as is the case with many of those in Kansas. The drilling derrick, complete with its machinery, is called a rig. A typical derrick may be as tall as a ten-story office building. The chief function of the rig is to drill the hole and raise and lower the drilling tools. Near the rig is a sump pit. In this pit is stored the liquid mud used in the well while drilling. The mud is a special mixture of clay, water, and a few other items.

When drilling starts, the drill begins to bore down with an action much like that of a brace and bit. The drilling is done by the drill stem, which consists of the drill pipe, drill collar, and bit. The most common type of bit used in Kansas is called a fishtail bit. It is not long until the hole is drilled to the depth of the drill pipe. The drilling is then stopped and another stand of pipe added. A stand is a number of joints of pipe. A joint is about twenty feet long. A stand is made up of two, three, or four joints. Extra stands are stacked inside the derrick ready for use. Stand after stand is added until the bit is worn and has to be changed. To change the bit, all the drill pipe has to be pulled from the hole.

During the drilling, the bit and drill pipe are turning in a bath of mud. The mud is pumped from the sump pit and forced, under pressure, through the mud hose into the pipe. As it goes down the pipe, it is forced through small holes in the bit and up the walls of the well to the surface, where it goes through the settling trough. Liquid mud cleans the well of its cuttings, keeps the bit cool, coats the walls of the well, and helps prevent caving. It also helps to seal off water zones.

Oil is found in porous rock formations or porous sands. The most famous oil-producing sand in Kansas is the Arbuckle. When oil men speak of an oil pool they do not mean that the oil is in a pool like a pool of water. They mean a porous rock formation with the spaces between the rocks filled with oil. When the oil-filled sand is struck, the drill is pulled from the well. New piping, called an oil string, is attached and lowered into the well. The upper end is connected with a valve and a pipeline system. The gas pressure in the well may force the oil to the surface. The well then begins to flow. If there is not enough natural pressure to force oil to the surface, the well is pumped. Many new wells now have to be pumped.

Sometimes the natural gas pressure is so strong that it causes a gusher. In 1917 the drillers in the El Dorado Field brought in a well that became a famous gusher. The gas was so strong that the roar it made could be heard for miles. It forced the oil up into the air over a hundred feet. Much equipment was destroyed and oil flowed over the ground. This well, which became known as the "Trapshooters Well," spouted 24,000 barrels of oil in one day. Only after a great amount of oil and gas had been lost, and after much damage had been done, was the well brought under control. Because the drillers know better how to control wells now, there are very few gushers.

It is believed that most of the possible oil-producing areas in Kansas have

An Oil Field in Stafford County. Petroleum is the principal mineral product of Kansas. Oil wells are a common sight on the landscape in many parts of the state. This field, a part of the Richardson Pool, is in Stafford County.

been discovered. The amount of Kansas's oil supply is not known. Several conservation laws have been passed. Only so much oil may be taken from a well in any given time. New methods are helping the companies get more oil from the older wells. In some places the wells are being drilled deeper in the hope of finding new oil sands. The deepest well drilled in Kansas is 7,912 feet, but the deepest production comes from 6,485 feet. Most wells are about 3,500 feet deep. More care is being used in storing the oil. As the amount of oil becomes less, the cost of its products will become greater.

Natural gas is often called the perfect fuel. Its production is closely related to the production of petroleum. Almost all gas wells have been brought in during the drilling for oil. Some fields, like the Hugoton Field in the southwestern part of the state produce only natural gas, but most fields produce both crude oil and gas. Most of the natural gas is used in homes and industry. Gas is the cheapest type of fuel one can buy. It is piped from the producing areas to many of the large cities in the eastern states. Kansas has an estimated gas reserve of about 19.3 trillion cubic feet and ranks fifth in gas production.

Coal, like petroleum, is a product of ages past. Coal is the remains of ancient forests and plants that have been preserved in the earth. When much of what is now eastern Kansas was covered by great inland seas and swamps, large forests stood on their banks. As the trees and plants died they fell into the swamps. Others grew up among the trunks and branches of the fallen vegetation, only in turn to die and fall into the swamps. This continued until there was a great mass of vegetation filling the swamps to depths of fifty to one hundred feet and covering hundreds of square miles in area. Streams flowing into these swamps filled them with mud, sand, and silt until finally the vegetation was covered hundreds of feet deep. With the increase in pressure and weight, certain parts of the old vegetation disappeared, leaving the carbon part of the plants. Finally the mass was changed into a substance known as peat. As the oceans and swamps continued to fill, more pressure and weight were added until a brown type of coal, called lignite, was formed. In the course of time more changes took place and the material finally became soft coal, or bituminous coal. Most of the coal mined in Kansas today is bituminous. During this time the original thickness of fifty to one hundred feet had been compressed until the coal beds were only three to six feet in thickness.

Coal is mined in several counties in the eastern part of the state, but production has declined rapidly in recent years. The Cherokee Plain and the Osage Cuestas are the chief regions of production (Map 29). The principal methods of mining coal in Kansas are called "shaft" mining and "strip" mining. *Shaft mining* is used to bring coal from the seams that are far underground. An elevator or cage takes the miners down the shaft into the mines. From the shaft, passageways extend in different directions. Coal is dug from rooms extending along the passageway. The thickness of the coal seams, or veins, varies from place to place even in the same mine. An undercutting machine cuts a long groove at the bottom of the wall of coal. Sometimes the miner must make this groove with a pickax. After the coal has been undercut, holes are drilled into the wall which the miner wants to break down. Explosives are put into these holes. If there is no dangerous gas in the room the shot is fired and larger chunks of coal are broken off. As the coal is taken

Kansas Industrial Development Commission

A Large Shovel Scooping Out Coal. Large shovels that scoop out many hundreds of pounds of coal at a time are used in the strip mines of the Cherokee Plain. Compare the size of the scoop with the size of the automobile.

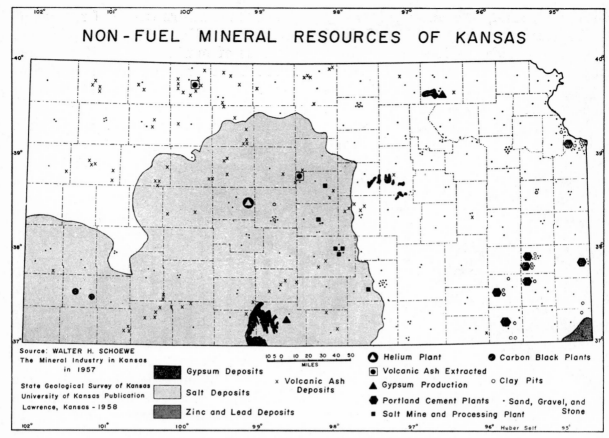

NON-FUEL MINERAL RESOURCES OF KANSAS

Source: WALTER H. SCHOEWE
The Mineral Industry in Kansas
in 1957

State Geological Survey of Kansas
University of Kansas Publication
Lawrence, Kansas - 1958

MILES
10 5 0   10 20 30 40 50

Gypsum Deposits

Salt Deposits

Zinc and Lead Deposits

x Volcanic Ash
Deposits

△ Helium Plant
◉ Volcanic Ash Extracted
▲ Gypsum Production
⬡ Portland Cement Plants
■ Salt Mine and Processing Plant

● Carbon Black Plants
○ Clay Pits
· Sand, Gravel, and
Stone

Huber Self

Map 28. Non-Fuel Mineral Resources of Kansas

out and the room gets larger, the miner must put in props to hold up the ceiling. Sometimes these props are wooden posts; sometimes columns of coal are left standing.

In some mines the miners load the chunks of coal into small cars which carry the coal to the shaft or entrance of the mine. In the large mines, mechanical loaders pick up the chunks of coal and fill the cars. In most mines today, electric motors pull the cars along the tracks through the low passageways of the mine.

The loaded cars are taken to a tall building called a *tipple*. In the tipple the coal is dumped on inclined chutes or slides. As the coal slides down, the pieces of slate and stone are taken out.

Sometimes this work is done by men, sometimes by machines. The coal is separated into different sizes by dropping through different size holes in the chute. Different sizes are sold under different names and for different purposes. The principal deep shaft mines of Kansas are in Crawford, Osage, and Cherokee counties.

In *strip mining* there are no shafts or underground passageways. The coal to be mined is near the surface. The soil covering the coal is scraped off by large machines and is piled to one side, leaving a coal floor. In some places as much as thirty to forty feet are removed before the coal is reached. Holes are drilled in the floor and filled with explosives. When the explosion takes place, it breaks the coal into pieces so that large mechanical scoops can pick it up and load it on trucks waiting nearby. The coal may then be hauled to a tipple where it is screened like the coal from a shaft mine. Large areas of strip mining are found in Linn, Crawford, Cherokee, and Bourbon counties.

Kansas produces about one million tons of coal per year, which is only about half that produced ten years ago. Of this amount, more than 90 per cent comes from strip mines. In an average year there are between thirty and forty coal mines operating. They employ about 360 persons a year.

Coal is one of the most useful products known to man. People often think of coal as only fuel, but there are about 2,500 different items made from it. Many chemicals and medicines are made of coal. Gasoline and oils can be made from coal. Even nylon is made partly of coal.

Kansas does not mine as much coal as previously. People prefer to use natural gas and fuel oil if they are available. It is estimated that Kansas has a coal reserve of a little over one billion tons. As the amount of oil produced decreases, coal production will increase.

Metals

Lead and zinc are the two principal metals mined in Kansas. The producing area is all in Cherokee County, or the Ozark Plateau Region. The lead and zinc mines in Kansas, Oklahoma, and Missouri are referred to as the Tri-State or Joplin District. Baxter Springs and Galena are the two chief cities of the region.

Lead and zinc are mined from shaft mines. Zinc is found in an ore called *sphalerite;* lead is taken from *galena* ore. These rocks exist in thick seams which are usually shallow, not going any deeper than 400 feet. After the

Kansas Industrial Development Commission

The Ozark Plateau is noted for its lead and zinc mines. Mountains of chat, some a hundred feet high, mark the location of mining activities in Cherokee County.

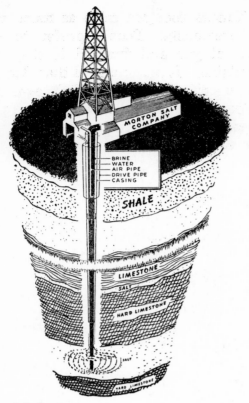

Morton Salt Company

Much salt is mined through wells. Feed water is put down the outside pipe; brine is brought up through the center pipe.

mine is worked out, it leaves a great system of underground caves.

When the ore is brought to the surface it is run through a mill where it is crushed and much of the waste product separated from the ore. Near each of the mills are large piles of waste called tailings, or *chat*. In recent years some of the tailing piles have been reworked and much good zinc recovered. Zinc ore is shipped to large smelters where the zinc is finally separated from the other materials. A large smelter is located in Galena.

Zinc is used for making many products. Steel items are often coated with a thin layer which keeps them from rusting. This is called *galvanizing*. Zinc plates form an important part of

storage batteries. Zinc is used in paints. Tubes and pipes can be made of zinc. All brass is partly zinc. Lead is also used in making pipes, some kinds of paints, and batteries. Lead is of special importance in the atomic industry. It is used in making containers for the material.

Nonmetals

Kansas has a wide variety of nonmetallic minerals. Many have been developed and are being used in local and national manufacturing. As the deposits of nonmetallic minerals in the more densely populated states are used, the demand for Kansas minerals will increase.

Salt is one of the great natural resources of Kansas. Much of the southwestern part of the state is underlain by salt. This mineral was deposited there long ago when western Kansas was covered by a great inland sea. Salt is mined by both the shaft and well methods.

Ellsworth, Reno, Rice, and Saline counties are the chief centers for production. Shaft mines are in operation near Kanopolis, Lyons, and Hutchinson. In these mines, a shaft is sunk into the ground to the desired level, which may be as much as 1,000 feet deep. Large chambers are then cut out to secure the salt. This is done with the use of machinery and explosives much as in a coal mine. After the salt has been broken from the walls, it is carried by train to elevators where it is lifted to the surface. The salt is then crushed and dried. Salt mined in this way is called rock salt.

Wells have been drilled in the same areas, and near the same cities, where

Mining Salt at Lyons. Some salt is mined by the shaft and tunnel method. Men operate large machines that dig out the rock salt and put it into large carriers.

shaft mines have been dug. In the well method, a small pipe is set inside a larger one. Very hot fresh water is pumped into the well through the larger pipe. The hot water dissolves the salt. Pressure forces the salt water back to the surface through the inner, smaller pipe. This salt water then is put into pans and the water evaporated. The salt is left.

Salt is used for many things. It is the only food man eats regularly that is not grown either directly or indirectly. Large quantities of salt are mixed with other minerals and sold for livestock salt. Much salt is used in the chemical industry. The total production of salt in Kansas amounts to over 900,000 tons per year. More rock salt than evaporated salt is produced.

Clay deposits are found in most parts of Kansas. Clay is a rather common product and cannot be shipped great distances unless the product to be made from it will bring a high price. Brick, tile, and pottery, are the most common products made of clay. Brick of various kinds are made in Buffalo, Great Bend, Neodesha, Coffeyville, Iola, Concordia, Humboldt, Kanopolis, Hoisington, and other large cities. Pottery products are made in plants at Hutchinson, Ellsworth, Pittsburg, and other places.

Gypsum is found in large quantities in the Red Hills Region and other parts of the state. Some of the deposits are in beds forty to sixty feet thick and several miles long. The uses made of gypsum depend upon its composition, for there are several grades of the mineral. The makers of cement use much crushed gypsum. Ground gypsum is used as a fertilizer, and as a filler in paint, paper, and cloth. Wallboard is made from gypsum in Medicine Lodge and plaster in Blue Rapids.

Sand and gravel form another large supply of natural resources. Kansas has large supplies of these minerals located in various sections of the state. These materials are used in large quantities for road building and concrete construction work. The value of these products amounts to over $5,000,000 a year.

Kansas has large quantities of limestone that are widely used in industry. Many public buildings in the state are made from cut limestone, much is used as crushed stone, and many tons are used annually for making Portland cement. Limestone quarries employ more than 850 persons, and the industry produces several millions of dollars worth of products annually.

Mineral Conservation

Minerals, like soil, water, and grass, need to be conserved. In fact, minerals need to be conserved more carefully than any of the others because minerals cannot be replaced. Grass can be replanted and it will grow again. Dams can be built and water stored for use when needed. Soil can be fertilized and, with care, made productive again. Once a mineral is mined and used, it is gone forever. The coal that is burned in the stove, the gasoline that makes the car go, are used only once. They cannot be used a second time. So it is with many other minerals.

Each mineral must be conserved in a different way. Substitutes may be found for some. New inventions may help save others. State and federal laws requiring wise use of all minerals

Huber Self

A Stone Quarry Two Miles North of Manhattan. This is Cottonwood limestone from which many public buildings in Kansas have been constructed. Most of the older buildings on Kansas State University Campus are constructed of Cottonwood limestone.

must be enforced. People must learn to care for what they have, for care will make all things last longer.

STUDENT ACTIVITIES

1. What minerals are produced in your county? Where are they sold? For what are they used?

2. How does Kansas compare with other states in the amount of petroleum produced? The amount of coal mined.

3. How do geologists believe coal and petroleum were formed?

4. Make a list of all the items you can name that are made entirely or partly from petroleum. Compare this list with that of your classmates. Why is petroleum such an important mineral?

5. What are the differences between metals and nonmetals? What are the principal metals mined in Kansas? The principal nonmetals?

6. Make a drawing to show some of the different kinds of places where petroleum may be found.

7. Can a mineral deposit be classed as a dependable and lasting resource? Why?

8. Locate the principal oil-producing areas in the state. Which is the greatest?

9. Why must minerals be conserved? How can this be done?

10. Name three minerals classed as mineral fuels. Name four minerals that are classed as metals. Name five minerals that are classed as nonmetals.

11. Can the mineral resources always play the large part that they now play in the trade of Kansas? Why?

Chapter 11

SERVICE INDUSTRIES OF KANSAS

The service industries are trade, transportation, and communication. These industries bring to Kansas products and news from the rest of the world. They also carry Kansas products and news from place to place within the state and to the rest of the world. In early days Kansas pioneers supplied their own needs largely without help from the outside world. In the modern age Kansas receives a wide variety of products from every part of the world. All of the tropical and subtropical food which is consumed must be purchased from other states or nations. The people of Kansas also buy large amounts of ready-made clothing, furniture, machinery, electrical equipment, drugs, paper, and other materials made outside the state. In order to buy these products Kansas sells agricultural products, minerals, and an increasing amount of manufactured goods.

Transportation and communication are important parts of the geography of Kansas. Products of the farms, ranches, and mines are of little use or value until they become usable goods. The movement of these goods to the manufacturing plants and then to the markets is the work of transportation units. Anything that is moved from one place to another is transported. In Kansas the chief methods of transportation are by car, bus, truck, train, and airplane. The movement of oil through pipelines and the movement of electricity over highlines are also methods of transportation.

Communication is the sending of messages, or information of any kind, from person to person or from place to place. The most common method of communication is people's talking with each other. The mails, telephone, telegraph, radio, television, and newspapers are all important methods of communication.

Many factors influence the development of the service industries in the various parts of the state. In regions having large populations all are found. In sparsely settled areas there may be only one or two kinds of each.

Transportation

The highway system of Kansas extends to all parts of the state. The principal part of the system is made up of approximately 73,950 miles of paved and improved roads. More than 18,200 miles of these roads have hard surfaces of blacktop or concrete. The Glaciated Region, Cherokee Plain, Osage Cuestas, and the Great Bend Prairie have more and better roads than the other regions. The number of oil fields, coal mines, good farms, and large cities in these regions makes it necessary that many good highways be built. The Chautauqua Hills and Red Hills have the least mileage of improved roads.

The care and construction of highways is supported by local and state taxes. The Federal Government also helps pay the cost on roads known as U.S. Highways. Road work and building is under the supervision of the

Part of the Kansas Turnpike. This four-lane highway is 236 miles long. It is the fourth longest toll road in the United States.

State Highway Commission. In the last ten years many improvements have been made in all parts of the state. Improved and paved highways now extend through each county. Four-lane highways now lead into Wichita and Kansas City. Roads around Topeka, Lawrence, Salina, and other large cities, where the traffic is greatest, have also been improved and widened. Many new bridges have been built across the creeks and rivers. The Kansas Turnpike, about 245 miles in length, extends from Kansas City, past Lawrence, Topeka, and Wichita, and then south to the Oklahoma border.

All highways in Kansas are numbered. The number of a federal highway is usually enclosed in a shield. All north-south federal highways are numbered with uneven numbers; all east-west federal highways have even numbers. The most used north-south high-

ways are United States Highways numbered 81, 69, 75, and 77. United States Highways numbered 40, 50, 54, and 24 are the most important east-west roads across the state. There is always a great amount of traffic where these highways cross each other.

The number of a state highway is usually enclosed in a circle or an oval. The state highways are numbered in the same manner as the federal highways. Many of the principal state highways are in the western part of Kansas where they connect areas of few people. State Highway No. 99, however, extends north-south through the Flint Hills and serves an important eastern region.

Buses serve as an important means of transportation in Kansas. Thirty-two bus companies operate over the Kansas highways. Bus lines extend into many cities not served by railroads.

County seats such as Russell Springs, Gove City, Westmoreland, and Mound City have no other kind of passenger service. Buses also serve many other places in which trains do not stop. The greatest number of buses run in the parts of the state having the greatest population.

Trucking companies serve as important freight carriers in Kansas. There are about 2,300 companies using the highways of the state. They serve many towns and villages in Kansas that are not served by railroads. Especially are they of great value in hauling the lighter materials short distances

Railroads were first built into the eastern part of Kansas about 1860. Some of the first railroads were built across the state to aid in shipping cat-tle to market. Others were extended westward to serve the coal-mining and oil-producing areas. Many cities and towns got their start where railroads crossed. From this early start railroads have been built into all parts of the state. Kansas ranks fifth in the nation in railway mileage with a total of 8,416 miles of rail lines. Only the states of Illinois, Indiana, Ohio, and Pennsylvania have a greater mileage.

Railroads, like highways, are built where there is the greatest demand for their services. The eastern half of the state has a greater railroad mileage than the western. The High Plains, Smoky Hills, and the Red Hills have the least mileage for the area covered. In many parts of the state it has been necessary to abandon trackage. Railroads often build many extra miles of

A Railroad Shipping Yard in Atchison. Railroads play an important part in the business of each of the cities of Kansas. In the larger cities many miles of track service the various industries. This scene illustrates the importance of the railroad to the elevators and flour mills of Atchison.

Municipal Airport at Hutchinson. Many of the cities and towns of Kansas have modern airports and regularly scheduled airline stops. Notice the tower and the weather instruments on top of it. This is the Hutchinson Municipal Airport.

track in oil fields or mining areas to help carry necessary materials for production. When there is no longer need for them, the tracks are removed. Some railroads no longer carry passengers but move only freight. The building of good highways, and the use of private cars, buses, and trucks are causing the railroads to make these changes.

In 1959, there were sixteen railroads operating in Kansas over 8,416 miles of track. Eleven of these railroads— Atchison, Topeka, and Santa Fe (Santa Fe); Chicago, Burlington and Quincy (Burlington); Chicago Great Western; Chicago, Rock Island, and Pacific (Rock Island); Kansas City Southern; Kansas, Oklahoma, and Gulf; Mid-

land Valley; Missouri-Kansas-Texas (Katy); Missouri Pacific; St. Louis-San Francisco (Frisco); and Union Pacific—are rated as Class I. The other five railroads are shorter lines that serve only a small part of the state.

Railroad centers develop where important main lines cross. Wichita, Newton, Topeka, Salina, Kansas City, Pittsburg, and Dodge City are important shipping points for their parts of the state. They are also important transfer points for goods that travel over more than one rail line. Each has two or more different rail lines crossing in it. Numerous other places such as Winfield, Marysville, Emporia, Manhattan, Great Bend, and Hutchinson are also important rail centers. The newer, faster trains do not stop at all stations as trains once did. Improved cars, heavy diesel engines, and good roadbeds make the operation of trains very expensive. It is cheaper for the new trains to stop only at the principal centers. Slower trains make stops at the smaller places.

Airplanes are rapidly becoming an important part of the transportation system of Kansas. Wichita, Kansas City, Topeka, Hutchinson, and other cities are regular stops for airlines that fly planes to all parts of the United States and several foreign countries. Good airports have been built in many Kansas towns and cities. Both east and west coast cities can be reached within a few hours.

Aviation depends upon good flying weather, and Kansas has more good weather for flying than the average state. Large amounts of flat land are also necessary since large planes cannot land in small areas. Land that is away from ridges, hills, and tall buildings is desired. Because conditions are favorable for building airports, and the weather is good for flying, the Armed Services have training centers or facilities near Olathe, Salina, Topeka, and Wichita. Wichita is one of the leading centers of the nation for the manufacture and assembly of aircraft. The geographic conditions of Kansas are favorable for the future growth of airlines in the transportation of freight as well as passengers.

Water transportation serves the northeastern corner of the state. The Missouri River accommodates barges to Kansas City, Leavenworth, and Atchison. In 1955 this amounted to over 3,000,000 tons of river commerce. During recent years this commerce has decreased due to the silting of the river. Dredging of the Missouri River so that larger barges may use this waterway is now being considered.

Pipelines are used to transport crude oil, refined oil, and natural gas. A pipeline system is much like a railway system. It has feeder lines which gather the crude oil and deliver it to the main, or trunk, lines. The trunk lines transport the crude oil to the refining centers. In turn, other pipelines transport the refined product from the refinery to the market. Many large pipelines have been built from Kansas to the refineries in the northern and eastern states.

Oil and gas are pumped through the pipes. Pumps are an important part of a pipeline system. Pumping stations are located at intervals along the line. In the level parts of Kansas the pump stations are about forty miles apart. The pumps exert pressure which forces the oil through pipes to the next pumping station at a rate of about four and a half miles an hour. In the state there are about 14,765 miles of pipeline used for transporting oil, and approximately 24,150 miles for natural gas.

Electric highlines carry energy and power to all parts of Kansas. This power is used to light homes and stores, to furnish energy to run factories, and to help with many other small and large jobs. Plants in Kansas generate almost all the power used in the state. Each part of Kansas has several power plants. Most of the plants use natural gas or coal as the fuel for generating electricity. Some use oil. Only a few of the smaller dams are equipped to

A Steam Electrical Generating Plant. Coal and natural gas are both used in the generation of electricity. This is the exterior view of a powerhouse showing coal conveyor and coal silos used as a standby fuel source when natural gas is not available. This steam generating plant can produce a million pounds of steam an hour and enough electrical energy to last the average household 435 years.

generate small amounts of electricity by water power. Communities that do not generate their own electricity buy it from one of the commercial companies. About three fourths of the rural areas of Kansas have had power lines installed in the last twenty years. With electricity the farm areas have many of the advantages of the towns and cities.

Communication

Mail is one of the principal forms of business and personal communication. Post offices are located in all sections of the state. In many rural areas the post office occupies a small space in a general store. Rural carriers often deliver mail for many miles from these small offices. In the larger towns and cities the post office is a complete business function by itself. Mail is delivered directly to the homes in the cities and most of the larger towns. Trains, buses, private carriers, and airplanes are all used to transport mail.

Telephone service extends into all parts of Kansas. This service is best developed where population is greatest and there is a demand for telephones. In Kansas, 271 companies co-operate in furnishing service to 843,660 rural and urban subscribers. Over 3,000,000 miles of telephone lines are used by these companies.

The exchanges operated by the smaller companies connect with the main exchanges of the larger companies, giving excellent coverage to the state. Over the combined facilities of these companies, a person is able to talk to almost any place in the world.

Telegraph service is available in communities where railroads have agents. The larger cities and towns also have separate offices with messengers to deliver the telegrams. The telegraph messages are handled by the American Telegraph System and Western Union. These companies frequently lease lines from the telephone companies.

Radio and television are also very

important means of communication. Both are used to communicate with large audiences of people. There are several large broadcasting companies in America each of which has many outlets through the radio and television stations of Kansas. The larger stations broadcast with enough power so that their programs may be heard or seen many miles away.

Trade

Shops, stores, and other firms which sell directly to the consumer such merchandise as groceries, clothing, furniture, cars, gasoline, and drugs are called *retail stores*. This local business is called retail trade. There are about 25,000 stores of all kinds selling merchandise in Kansas. These stores sell about $2,590,000,000 worth of merchandise to the people of the state each year. This amounts to about $1,300 per person. The total retail sales for the United States is about 175 billion dollars per year or a little over $1,000 per person.

Much of this large sum is spent for food and drink. Grocery stores account for most of the sales of foods, but there are many other kinds of food and drink shops such as meat markets, sea-food markets, fruit and vegetable stores, candy and nut stores, bakeries, and restaurants. The retail stores and shops sell about $600,000,000 yearly in foods, which is 27 per cent of the total retail sales. In 1958 there were about 4,500 grocery stores in Kansas, which is about 16 per cent of all retail establishments.

There are many other groups of important retail establishments. General clothing stores which sell dry-goods, clothing, boots and shoes, and millinery are especially important. The automobile dealers sell products worth over $500,000,000 each year. In addition to automobiles they sell parts, motorcycles, and trailers. Gasoline stations are to be found in all sections of the state. A variety of stores sell jewelry, books, flowers, camera supplies, and numerous other items, and employ many people.

The managers and proprietors of these retail stores form one of the most important groups of professional people in Kansas. To serve their customers they handle good products from all parts of the world. It is necessary for these people to be keen business men.

There are many factors to be considered in the retail business. A chain grocery store may invest as much as $325,000 in building and stock before it is ready to open. Such a large investment requires careful planning and management to insure profits. The store may handle about 12,000 sales a week at an average of $6.50 per sale. Such a store, therefore, sells to its customers $78,000 in groceries in a week, and $4,056,000 in gross sales in a year. The manager buys from local producers such items as dairy products, some meat and poultry products, vegetables when in season, some flour, and baked goods. His groceries come mainly from large wholesale houses in Wichita and Kansas City. A look at the shelves of the store shows that any one store must depend upon a warehouse where the produce is collected from over the United States and the world. Just a few of the goods gathered from many places are shoe polish from Brooklyn, plastic containers from Detroit, soaps from Cincinnati, furniture polish from

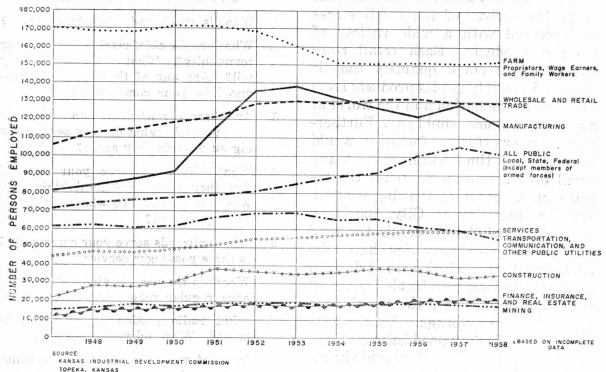

KANSAS EMPLOYMENT PATTERN 1948-1958

NUMBER OF PERSONS EMPLOYED

FARM
Proprietors, Wage Earners, and Family Workers

WHOLESALE AND RETAIL TRADE

MANUFACTURING

ALL PUBLIC
Local, State, Federal (except members of armed forces)

SERVICES

TRANSPORTATION, COMMUNICATION, AND OTHER PUBLIC UTILITIES

CONSTRUCTION

FINANCE, INSURANCE, AND REAL ESTATE

MINING

ˣBASED ON INCOMPLETE DATA

SOURCE:
KANSAS INDUSTRIAL DEVELOPMENT COMMISSION
TOPEKA, KANSAS

Kansas Employment Pattern 1948-1958

What Kansas People Do for a Living. A study of this chart will show the most important occupations in Kansas.

Chicago, floor wax from Racine, candy from Philadelphia and New York, deep-fry cottonseed oil from Memphis, cranberries from Boston, catsup from San Francisco. There are many brands of these products; the local manager learns the tastes of his customers and provides for them.

The manager of a department store has an even bigger task since he cannot depend on one warehouse alone to provide his merchandise. He must travel widely and have buying contacts in many cities. It is necessary for him to know the quality and fix the prices on a wide variety of wearing apparel, household furnishings and equipment, and many other different articles. One large store employs 150 sales people

and other helpers. It accommodates an average of 15,000 customers a week or a total of 780,000 customers a year. These customers buy about $3,000,000 in merchandise per year. In order to supply them the manager and his buyers visit the large display centers in New York, Chicago, St. Louis, and other places which display and manufacture department store wares. Often a local manager will inform a resident buyer in some city of his needs. This buyer will then make such contacts as will enable the local manager to see displays of the goods he desires. The resident buyer gives the manager the benefit of his vast buying power which may be as much as $1,000,000,000 a year.

115

Wholesale trade is the business that keeps the shelves of the retail stores well stocked with a wide variety of low-cost products. Each retail store buys in such small quantity that it could not possibly get its products from all parts of the nation and the world at a cost the customer could pay. Furthermore, transportation facilities would have a hard time handling so many small orders coming from all the retail stores. Instead, two big centers, Wichita and Kansas City, handle a large share of the wholesale trade of Kansas. These two cities have the transportation facilities to bring in products in any desirable quantity from anywhere. Also the warehouses have space for storage. Transportation connections are good between these two large wholesale centers and the retail markets of the state.

The wholesale trade in Kansas for a year is about $2,000,000,000. Of course, retail stores buy from sources other than Kansas wholesale markets; on the other hand, many retailers sell to people living outside the state. Although wholesale stores are widely distributed over the state, not every county has a wholesale center.

STUDENT ACTIVITIES

1. What is retail trade? Wholesale trade?

2. What are the chief retail stores of your community? What products do they sell? Are any of these products produced in your community?

3. Are there any wholesale stores in your community? What do they sell? How big an area do they serve?

4. What highways serve your county? Are they state or federal highways? Are they paved? To what large cities do they extend?

5. What railroads serve your community? Is there passenger service?

6. Where is the nearest airport? Does it have regular scheduled airline stops?

7. What radio station is nearest your home? What television station?

8. In what ways do good lines of transportation help a community?

9. What are the principal railroads, airlines, and highways crossing Kansas?

10. Is your home community on a navigable waterway? Why is water transportation confined to the northeastern corner of the state?

Chapter 12

MANUFACTURING

Manufacturing is changing raw products of the farms, ranches, and mines into usable goods. When wheat is changed into flour, or crude oil into gasoline, or milk into ice cream, manufacturing has taken place. Almost all the food we eat and all the clothing we wear have been changed by some process of manufacturing. Manufacturing plants are of many sizes. They do not have to be large buildings, with many machines, that have hundreds of people working in them. A small bakery that employs only one or two persons is as much a manufacturing plant as is a large bakery that employs many persons.

Kansas is more of a producer of raw materials than it is of manufactured goods. Many of the crops grown, and much of the minerals mined, are shipped to other states to be made into usable goods. The factories of Kansas vary a great deal in size. Most of them are small and manufacture such items as butter, bread, and newspapers which are used in the local community. There are some plants, however, like the large flour mills, oil refineries, and airplane factories that employ many hundreds of persons and sell their goods in all parts of the United States and in other countries.

There is manufacturing of some kind in every county in the state. The largest number of manufacturing plants are in the cities and counties that have the largest populations. A plant may have been located in a town because of the number of people living there. In some cases people move into a town to get work in one of its factories. Most large factories must have a large supply of labor. A good supply of fuel, rapid transportation and communication, good schools, modern churches, a large supply of fresh water, and a healthful climate are also factors that are considered.

Food Manufacturing

Changing raw agricultural products into usable foods is one of the most important industries in Kansas. This type of manufacturing is found in all parts of the state. Many of the plants are small and employ only a few people. Most of their products are used in the town in which the factory is located. Some small plants put out special products like potato chips, peanut butter, honey, nut meats, and extracts that are sold in all parts of the state. The large food-processing plants, like the large flour mills, canneries, and meat-packing plants, are located in the larger towns and cities. They employ many workers and ship their products to various parts of the world.

Flour milling is the process by which wheat is made into flour. In Kansas there are forty-two flour mills. Most of the mills are located in the central part of the state near the eastern edge of the wheat-growing areas. Wichita is the state's largest flour-milling center; there are five mills in the city. Newton and Salina each have four flour mills, Abilene has three mills, and two mills are located in each of these cities:

Girls Hand-Breaking Eggs at Marysville Plant. The production of foods requires the services of many people. The people shown working here are "hand-breaking" eggs. The eggs are then prepared for shipment.

Arkansas City, Great Bend, Hutchinson, Topeka, Atchison, and McPherson.

Each month the flour mills in Kansas make about 4,166,667 bushels of wheat, or 50,000,000 bushels each year, into flour. The purpose of milling is to separate the flour part of the wheat seed from its outer coat of bran. Before entering the actual milling process, the grain is dry-cleaned and scoured. All bits of dust and dirt which have clung to it through the threshing and binning processes are removed. After cleaning, washing, and tempering, the wheat passes through steel grinders called the first break rolls. At this stage the flaky pieces of bran and crushed white floury part are all in one mixture. By a continuous process involving many grindings, siftings, and separations, the floury part is entirely cleaned of all bran parts. After being finely ground and forced through a close-meshed silk screen, it is packed as pure white flour. When ready for packing, the best white flours have gone through about 180 separations. In the course of the milling process, other products such as whole wheat flour and shorts, a livestock feed, have been manufactured. Sixty pounds of wheat usually produce forty-two pounds of white flour and eighteen pounds of bran and shorts.

Most of the flour used by the people of Kansas is made in Kansas. Kansas flour is also sold in many other states, for the mills produce much more flour than is needed to supply the people of the state.

Bakeries are the principal users of flour. Flours are manufactured for every baking purpose. The best cake flour is not good for making bread, and a good bread flour will not produce the best cakes. The principal product of

A Large Flour Mill in Hutchinson. Kansas is the leading wheat-producing state in the United States. Elevators for the storing of wheat are located in most parts of the state.

bakeries is white bread, the most common food in the United States.

Almost all the work in the large bakeries is done by machines. Large machines mix the flour with the other items used in making bread. After kneading, the dough is cut into chunks and weighed before being put into a

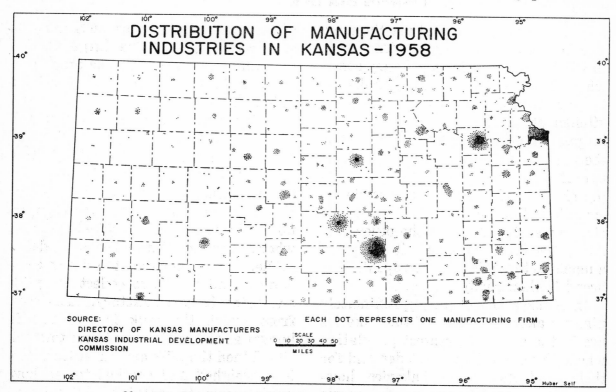

DISTRIBUTION OF MANUFACTURING INDUSTRIES IN KANSAS – 1958

SOURCE:
DIRECTORY OF KANSAS MANUFACTURERS
KANSAS INDUSTRIAL DEVELOPMENT
COMMISSION

EACH DOT REPRESENTS ONE MANUFACTURING FIRM

SCALE
0 10 20 30 40 50
MILES

Huber Self

Map 29. Distribution of Manufacturing Industries in Kansas, 1958

119

A Hog-Dressing Line in a Meat-Packing Plant. Washed, de-haired carcasses move in at the left and back at the right, where federal inspectors check the meat.

pan. Loaves of bread that are the same size have the same weight. The ovens in which the bread is baked vary somewhat. The oven used by many bakeries is very much like the oven in a regular kitchen stove except that it is much larger. In others the bread is baked as the pan moves through the oven. The pan of dough is placed on a slow-moving chain belt. The belt moves slowly enough so that the bread is baked just right when it comes out the other end. After the bread is baked, it is put in a machine that slices and wraps it. The bread is then ready for sale.

In Kansas there are approximately ninety bakeries. Most of the bakeries are in the areas of greatest population where there is the greatest demand for their products. Many bakeries, however, are located in the smaller towns

of the state. Bakery products must be sold while fresh. The large baking companies have many trucks that carry their products to the small communities daily.

Dairy products are those items which are manufactured from milk. Butter, cheese, and ice cream are the better known products, but there are several others. Since the success of manufacturing these products depends upon milk, the plants are located in areas where there are large herds of dairy cattle. Each morning the dairy companies send trucks to collect the milk and bring it to the factory. The area from which the milk is gathered is known as the milkshed of that town or city. When the milk arrives at the plant it is weighed and checked to see how much cream it contains. All milk is

Armour and Company

Armour and Company Plant, Kansas City. A large meat-packing plant is made up of several different units. In addition to the killing and dressing of the animals there are many different meat by-products made. This Armour and Company packing plant is one of the larger plants in the nation.

pasteurized before being made into the various products.

Butter is the most widely used of the dairy products and the principal product of most plants. There are forty-seven creameries in Kansas where butter is made. The plants located in Arkansas City, Topeka, Ottawa, Hillsboro, Dodge City, Concordia, Sabetha, and Kansas City are all large, each employing over 100 persons. There is about the same demand for butter all year. It can be stored for long periods of time. Kansas ships many pounds of butter to the densely populated eastern states.

Factories for making ice cream are located in all sections of the state, but the largest ones are in Kansas City, Wichita, and Topeka. Condensed and

evaporated milk are prepared in twenty-five Kansas factories and cheese of various kinds is produced in fifty-three. Ninety-two plants make and sell various other dairy products such as whipping cream, chocolate milk, buttermilk, and fresh milk. Some of the large factories produce all kinds of dairy products.

Meat-packing is one of the principal industries of the state. Kansas City, Kansas, along with Kansas City, Missouri, is one of the chief meat-packing centers of the nation. Seven different meat-packing plants in Kansas City employ over 100 persons each. Three large plants are located in Wichita. Topeka and Arkansas City also have packing plants that have more than 100 workers. The large stock yards and shipping pens are found in most cities and towns. Kansas is a natural place for the meat-packing industry to build. The large ranches in the Flint Hills, High Plains, Red Hills, and other areas all produce many hundreds of good beef cattle. Many small farmers have a few beef cattle to sell each year. Large numbers of hogs are also available. Sheep to supply mutton needs are also raised in Kansas.

Fresh meat products are the most important items of the meat-packing industry. No part of the animal is wasted. Dried beef, canned meats of various kinds, lard, hides and skins, tallow, soap stock, and dried-bone meal are just a few of the many products. Almost all of the nonmeat items are shipped from the state. Much fresh meat is sent to the large cities in the eastern states since Kansas produces more than it can use. For many years the reputation of Kansas meat has caused customers to ask for it in restaurants and cafes.

Sugar was manufactured in a large plant in Garden City. The Garden City company sold this plant to the Holly Sugar Corporation, and the beets are now transported to Holly, Colorado, for processing. Since 1956 the factory buildings have been used as a sugar warehouse for the Holly Corporation. The principal steps in the sugar-making process include washing the beets, slicing them into thin strips called *cossettes*, extracting the sugar in liquid form by "cooking" the cossettes in hot water, purifying the resulting thin juice, filtering it, evaporating, crystallizing, separating the crystals from the remaining syrup, and drying before packaging.

Products Manufactured from Minerals

Minerals, like agricultural products, are of little value until they are manufactured into usable goods. Kansas does not manufacture as many of its minerals as it should. Too many carloads of metals and nonmetals and too many barrels of crude oil are shipped to other states for processing. The manufacturers in other states buy the raw minerals very cheap, manufacture them, then sell the products made. This gives the manufacturers in other states a good profit for making Kansas minerals usable. If Kansas would process its own minerals, it would give work to many people and bring money into the state.

Petroleum products are the principal manufactured mineral goods. Crude oil is shipped from the tank farms by either pipeline, tank car, or truck to the refineries. In Kansas there are about fourteen refineries that make petroleum products as well as sixteen natural gasoline plants. Eleven of the refineries are located in the southeastern part of the state, three being in or near Wichita and El Dorado; Arkansas City, Coffeyville, and Chanute have two each. Eight of the natural gasoline plants are in the southwestern part of Kansas, five being in or near Ulysses.

Gasoline is the most valuable petroleum product. Refineries try to make a barrel of crude oil produce as many gallons of gasoline as possible. To do this, the oil is first put through a process called *fractionating*. This means that the crude oil is divided into many parts. The oil, as it is pumped to the fractionating tower, is heated in the pipes. As the oil becomes hotter, it

Skelly Oil Company

A Petroleum Refinery. A petroleum refinery is a large and complicated plant. A large tank farm is shown at the left; at the right is a Butane sphere. In the plant itself crude oil is processed and gasoline made. The refinery was established in 1917. The city of El Dorado is shown in the background.

turns into vapor, much as boiling water turns into steam. Some vapors are lighter than others and rise to the top of the tower. Some vapors are so heavy that they settle to the bottom. The lightest vapors go out of the tank through pipes at the top, while heavier vapors go out through the lower pipes. These vapors are cooled and form different products. Some of the products are again heated and put through another process known as *cracking*. By this process more gasoline and other oil products are formed.

For a refinery to work successfully, it must have many parts. There is a machine department to make repairs, a welding department, a department which cleans pipes, an electricity generating plant, a cooler plant, and a boiler department. Laboratories to check the crude oil before it is refined, and to check the refined product are also important.

One of the largest refineries in Kansas is located in El Dorado. Most of the oil comes to this refinery by pipeline from the fields in Kansas. After refining, the petroleum products are shipped out in tank cars and truck transports as well as through pipelines. From this plant the refined products are sent to places throughout the central and eastern states.

Portland cement is manufactured in large plants located in Bonner Springs, Chanute, Fredonia, Humboldt, Independence, and Iola. The principal material from which cement is made is limestone. All of the above-named plants, except the one in Bonner Springs, are located in the Osage Cuestas Region and secure their limestone from the rocks of that area. The stone is crushed, mixed with other materials, heated to very high temperatures inside great kilns (ovens), then crushed again and put through other processes that make it finally into cement.

Different kinds of cement are made for different purposes. Some cement is made just for oil wells; some is made for various kinds of construction work. Kansas cement is shipped to many states in the Mississippi River valley area.

Stone, clay, and gypsum products are also manufactured in Kansas. Brick, hollow tile, and pottery products are made from clay. Of the eleven brick and tile plants within the state, seven are located in the southeastern corner in the cities of Weir, Coffeyville, Neodesha, Fredonia, Buffalo, Humboldt, and Iola. The other four are in the north central part of Kansas. All are large plants for each employs more than fifty persons. Nine small pottery factories make such products as ceramics, stoneware, flower pots, and various other kinds of pottery.

Stone is used in making cement blocks, ready-mixed concrete, vaults, silos, and in numerous construction activities. There are approximately 120 plants of this type scattered over the state. Most are small, employing fewer than twenty-five full-time employees.

Gypsum products are made in factories located in Blue Rapids and Medicine Lodge. The Blue Rapids plant specializes in plaster of various kinds. A variety of products such as wall-board, Keene's cement, and wall plaster are made in the Medicine Lodge plant. This plant is large, employing over 100 persons.

Salt is prepared for market in factories located in Hutchinson, Kanopolis, and Lyons. The larger factories purify salt and clean the salt mined nearby. Most of it is packed as edible salt for use in bakeries, homes, canneries, or wherever needed in the preparation of foods. Some also prepare rock salt for use in the livestock industry. Kansas salt is used throughout the nation.

Transportation Equipment

Kansas is an important center for the production of transportation equipment of all kinds. Truck and passenger car trailers are manufactured in many parts of the state. More than thirty-five factories, almost all of them small, make truck and bus bodies. Farm wagons are made in Kingman and wagon beds are manufactured in

State Geological Survey of Kansas

A Cement Plant in Fredonia, Kansas. Cement is one of the most important of the building products. Limestone is the chief item used in its manufacture. The plant shown here has been in operation since 1905 and is located in Fredonia.

Beech Aircraft Corporation

An Assembly Line of Airplanes. The assembly of airplanes differs a great deal from that of automobiles. Here the planes are assembled in one place and not on a moving belt line.

Strong City, Valley Falls, and Independence. Almost as many people are employed in manufacturing and assembling transportation equipment as in all other types of manufacturing combined. The annual payroll for this kind of work is over five times as large as the next manufacturing group (Table 9).

Aircraft production and assembly are among the more important industries of the state, and Wichita is recognized as one of the principal aircraft centers of the nation. Four enormous plants that make aircraft are located in Wichita and one is located in Pittsburg. Factories of this type require much space both inside and outside the buildings. Many planes are assembled at the same time and in the same large rooms. The men who do each part of the work are specialists so they move from one plane to the other as they work; thus, many planes are being made at the same time. Some of these plants have people at work twenty-four hours each day and seven days a week. One of the largest planes made in the United States, a large airforce bomber, is made in Wichita. Aircraft engines, aircraft parts, and equipment are made in about sixty other factories located in various cities; over half of the factories are in Wichita. Most of these plants are much smaller than the aircraft assembly plants.

Railroad equipment such as boxcars, locomotive parts, railroad wheels, refrigerator cars, tank cars, and railroad equipment are made in factories in Wichita, Topeka, Kansas City, Argonia, Atchison, Parsons, Coffeyville, and Ellis. Some of the factories are owned by the railroads, but some make goods and sell to any railroad wanting to buy. Most of these plants employ over 100 persons.

Automobile assembly is an important

General Motors Corporation

An Aerial View of the General Motors Plant in Kansas City. Notice the size of the plant and the hundreds of automobiles parked about it. Some are completed new cars; others are cars belonging to the people that work in the plant.

industry in Kansas City. The one large plant there employs many hundreds of persons and assembles three makes of cars. Work in this factory differs greatly from that in an aircraft factory. Here the men work in the same general location all day and the material moves by them on an endless belt, or an assembly line. At one end of this constantly moving line the workers start to assemble a car. As it moves along, a body, engine, wheels, seats, windows, and other parts of the car are added. At the opposite end from where the assembling starts, a completed car rolls off the assembly line. From this factory, automobiles are sent to all parts of Kansas and many of the nearby states. "Made in Kansas" could be applied to many of our automobiles.

Other Manufactures

In addition to the manufactured goods already studied, the factories of Kansas make a variety of other items. In many cases the smaller factories operate only a part of the year and all of the work is done by the owner and his family. The larger factories operate twenty-four hours each day and the workers may live several miles from their work. The smaller factories usually sell their products in their own community or in neighboring communities. The products of the larger factories are sold in all parts of the world. Both the large and the small factories are important to Kansas. Both give employment to some of the state's people, and both bring money into the state.

Spencer Chemical Company

A Large Chemical Plant near Pittsburg. Chemicals are becoming more and more important in the life of the United States.

The small factories make many products. A factory in Marysville makes dentures. Wood gifts are made in Americus. Soft drinks are bottled in Beloit and many other towns in the state. Coal-washing is done at Hallowell. Feed is ground in Neodesha, Wolfe, Concordia, and Cherryvale. Many towns and cities have mattress factories. In some of the towns and cities near lakes, fishing lures are manufactured. Brooms are made in Douglass. Halstead has a plant that makes combine canvases. A large chemical plant is located in Pittsburg. Many towns have small factories producing jelly, jams, and candy.

Printing and publishing industries are among the most widespread industries in the state. Each county has at least one weekly newspaper or job printing shop. Each of the larger cities and several of the smaller ones have daily newspapers. Papers published in Wichita, Kansas City, and Topeka are delivered to all parts of the state. Book and magazine publishers have plants located in Topeka, Girard, Lawrence, Wichita, Hutchinson, Kansas City, and other places. Almost all of the paper, type, and machinery used in the publishing business are manufactured in other states.

Iron and steel products are manufactured in Dodge City, Arkansas City, Atchison, Coffeyville, Fort Scott, Pittsburg, Wichita, and several other cities of the state. Pig iron and iron plate are shipped into Kansas from blast furnaces in the eastern and southern states. Here the material is shaped and made into the kind of steel products needed. Truck springs, tank cars, oil-field tools, and water tanks are but a few of the items manufactured.

Rubber tires and tubes are made in large plants at Topeka and Hutchinson. The raw rubber and most of the material mixed with it are shipped into the state. The materials are cooked; then they are molded by heat and pressure into the shape desired. Tires made in these plants are sold in all parts of the United States.

Kansas now has more than 3,300 manufacturers. These factories employ over 130,000 persons per year and have an annual payroll of approximately $480,000,000, or almost 20 per cent of the total income for the state. The amount gained by the state as a result of the value added amounts to over one billion dollars a year. Because Kansas is a good location for the development of manufacturing, an average of over 100 new industries are coming into the state each year.

No longer can it be said that Kansas is just an agricultural state. Today manufacturing is as important as agriculture and, in the future, the state will also be recognized for its importance in manufacturing. Factories will bring more wealth and people.

TABLE 9

MAJOR MANUFACTURING INDUSTRIES IN KANSAS, 1957

TYPE OR KIND	AVERAGE NUMBER OF EMPLOYEES	MILLIONS OF DOLLARS ANNUAL PAYROLL
Apparel and other finished products	3,000	7.9
Chemicals and allied products	7,300	34.6
Dairy products	2,000	7.3
Grain mill products	4,500	16.9
Machinery	10,600	42.7
Meat products	9,100	43.6
Metals industries	7,800	32.7
Petroleum and coal products	5,200	28.8
Printing and publishing	8,300	35.9
Stone, clay, and glass products	5,900	24.7
Transportation equipment	54,800	258.0

The *Wichita Beacon*

Two Pressmen Inspecting Proof Copies of the Wichita Beacon. The eight-unit Goss Press prints over thirty-seven million individual copies of the Wichita Beacon each year.

STUDENT ACTIVITIES

1. What advantages does Kansas have for manufacturing activities? What disadvantages?

2. Why do the larger cities lead in manufacturing? Make a list of the chief products made in each.

3. In what ways have machines changed the output of plants? Why?

4. What are the principal manufacturing activities in your community? What raw materials are used? Where are the manufactured goods sold?

5. Make a collection of goods, or pictures of the goods, manufactured in Kansas. Arrange them in a display case or attach them to a map to show where they are made.

6. Which natural region has the greatest number of manufacturing activities? Why? Which has the least? Why?

7. In what ways does Kansas agriculture aid Kansas manufacturing?

8. How many of the things you have used today, such as food, clothing, transportation to school, and pencils, were probably made in Kansas? How many probably contain Kansas materials?

Chapter 13

PLAYGROUNDS OF KANSAS

It is just as necessary to conserve people as it is to conserve soil, minerals, and water. People in all types and all kinds of work need places where they can relax, rest, and enjoy themselves. Especially do people who do work in factories and offices need places where they can live and play in the fresh air and sunshine for a period of time each year. Not all people like the same kind of recreation. Some prefer to hunt, or fish, or hike. Others may want a vacation near a lake that has good sandy beaches and good swimming areas. Many people like best to drive from place to place and visit the various parts of the state.

In Kansas many recreational areas have been developed to meet the vacation needs of the people. Recently the

TABLE 10

KANSAS STATE PARKS AND LAKES

COUNTY	NEAREST TOWN OR CITY	ACRES IN		COMMENTS
		PARK	LAKE	
Allen-Bourbon	Elsmore	394	103	Heavily wooded park area
Atchison	Effingham	248	66	Equipped with extensive day-use facilities
Barber	Medicine Lodge	197	77	Fishing
Brown	Hiawatha	189	62	Spring-fed lake, fishing, picnicking
Butler #1	Augusta	568	232	Fishing, swimming, camping
Butler #2	Latham	351	124	Fishing
Chase	Cottonwood Falls	492	109	Being developed
Clark	Kingsdown	1,243	337	Bluff Creek Canyon, fishing, picnicking
Cowley	Arkansas City	197	80	Panther Creek Canyon, picnicking
Crawford #1	Pittsburg		60	Lakes are old strip pits, reforested area
Crawford #2	Farlington	460	150	Scenic wooded drives, federal fish hatchery
Decatur #1	Oberlin	92	47	Lake dry part of time, picnicking
Decatur #2	Oberlin	481	161	Fishing, picnicking, camping
Finney	Kalvesta	852	324	Waterfowl attraction, picnicking
Grant	Ulysses	224	44	Fishing, picnicking
Hamilton	Syracuse	432	94	Picnic and day-use facilities
Hodgeman	Jetmore	254	85	Fishing
Jewell	Mankato	165	57	Being developed
Kearny	Lakin		3,000	Fishing, hunting, picnicking
Kingman	Kingman		180	Camping, game reserve
Leavenworth	Tonganoxie	1,562	175	Fishing, boating, camping
Lyon	Reading	506	135	Fishing, camping, picnicking
Logan	Russell Springs	582	75	Fishing, day camping
McPherson	Canton	271	46	Fishing, boating, camping
Meade	Meade		100	Variety of scenery, game reserve
Miami	Paola	1,240	90	Heavily forested, fishing, picnicking
Montgomery	Independence	227	105	Fishing, camping, boating
Nemaha	Seneca	408	356	Swimming, fishing, camping
Neosho	Parsons	705	92	Oldest park, swimming, fishing, camping
Osage	Topeka	506	140	Being developed
Ottawa	Salina	711	138	Fishing, picnicking, camping, swimming
Pottawatomie #1	Westmoreland	100	24	Fishing, picnicking, camping
Pottawatomie #2	Manhattan	247	75	Camping, fishing
Republic	Jamestown	1,064	765	Lake shallow, dries up in drought
Rooks	Stockton	222	67	Fishing, picnicking, camping
Scott	Scott City	1,280	155	Picturesque scenery, historical importance
Sheridan	Quinter	436	124	Picnic facilities, fishing
Wilson	Yates Center	291	119	Being developed
Woodson	Toronto	445	179	Wooded area, camping, boating, fishing

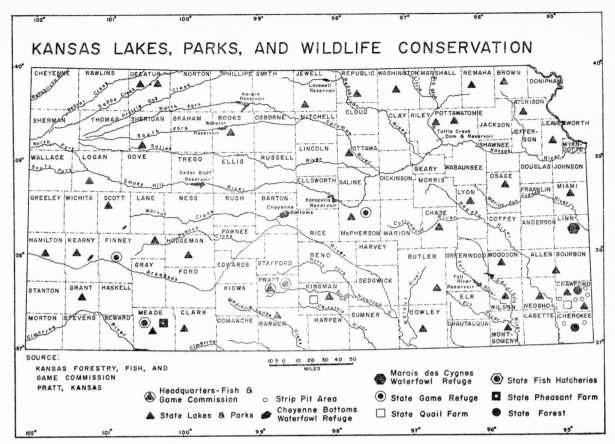

KANSAS LAKES, PARKS, AND WILDLIFE CONSERVATION

SOURCE:
KANSAS FORESTRY, FISH, AND
GAME COMMISSION
PRATT, KANSAS

10 5 0   10 20 30 40 50
MILES

◉ Headquarters–Fish & Game Commission
▲ State Lakes & Parks

⬡ Marais des Cygnes Waterfowl Refuge
◉ State Game Refuge
▢ State Quail Farm

○ Strip Pit Area
⬡ Cheyenne Bottoms Waterfowl Refuge

◎ State Fish Hatcheries
▣ State Pheasant Farm
● State Forest

Map 30. Kansas Lakes, Parks, and Wildlife Conservation

state and federal governments have built several dams which caused large lakes to form. The state government has developed thirty-nine state parks in various sections of the state. Many cities and towns have also developed parks and recreational areas for their people. In some parts of the state, individuals have built recreational and resort areas which serve many people each year.

Park Facilities

State parks furnish the people much enjoyment. The most useful parks are those that meet at least two requirements—good scenery or other interests, and nearness to many people. A small picnic ground that can be enjoyed several times during the summer is more valued by most people than a great park visited only once in a lifetime.

The Kansas recreation system contains many fine properties. The many state parks, lakes, and monuments supervised by the Kansas Forestry, Fish, and Game Commission are well placed and easily reached by the people of Kansas (Map 30). They range in size from 24 acres up to the 1,562-acre park eight miles west of Kingman on United States Highway No. 54.

Entry to the parks is free, but a small fee is charged for some of the services provided. More than 1,000,000 people visit the state parks each year.

131

Lake Shawnee near Topeka. Water sports are popular on Lake Shawnee near Topeka, Kansas.

The Kansas Highway Department fosters recreation in several ways. Many roadside parks are spaced along the highways. Each park usually contains shade trees or a shelter and picnic tables, and may have fireplaces and a water supply or other facilities. The Highway Department does a great deal to make the routes attractive. A wide right of way is owned by the state. In most places it is graded and grass-covered. Where possible, native trees have been preserved and additional trees or shrubs planted. Turnouts are provided at especially good scenic views so that they can be safely enjoyed.

City parks are owned by most Kansas cities. These parks are designed chiefly to serve their own people but attract visitors as well. Some of the larger cities have many smaller neighborhood parks such as the Quindaro, Clifton, and Heath Wood in Kansas City; McKinley, College Hill, and Fair-mont in Wichita; and Gage, Children's, and Ripley in Topeka. Frequently towns and cities make use of some natural feature for recreational areas. Wichita has developed Oak Park, Sun Memorial Park, and Central Riverside Park along the banks of the Arkansas or Little Arkansas rivers. Two parks in Salina—Oakdale and Kentwood—have been developed in meanders of the Smoky Hill River. Zoos are to be found not only in the larger cities but also in some of the smaller places such as Independence, Garden City, and Dodge City.

Tourist Attractions

For those who are not especially interested in sports and other outdoor activities, Kansas has much to offer in scenic beauty and historical places. Several tours will carry the traveler through beautiful ranch country in the Flint Hills, rich farmlands in the High

132

Plains, or interesting mining areas in Ozark Plateau or the Cherokee Plain. Many *cultural* areas are to be found in the state.

Several Kansas towns celebrate a special day or hold a fair as an annual attraction. These may serve to publicize some local product such as the Southeast Kansas Milking Shorthorn Show at Independence, Sedgwick County National Livestock Show at Wichita, and flower shows at Concordia, Sylvia, Leavenworth, Colby, Rexford, and many other places. Numerous county fairs are held during the late summer and early fall months. The annual official State Fair at Hutchinson attracts thousands of persons. The fair held in Topeka each year is also of state-wide interest.

Abilene is an important tourist center in Kansas. It was one of the early "cow towns" and has many historical places connected with its early activities. On the post office lawn is a boulder which marks the end of the Chisholm Trail over which thousands of cattle were driven. The Eisenhower home and museum attracts hundreds of tourists each year. The museum houses a vast collection of souvenirs, medals, trophies, and other personal tokens that belonged to President Eisenhower or the Eisenhower family. The building stands on a part of the original farm. Many historical markers have been placed about the city to show the location of numerous past events.

Dodge City, another "cow town," also has much history connected with it that attracts tourists. The Santa Fe Trail passed near the city, and west of Dodge City was the location of the

Kansas Industrial Development Commission

Scott County State Park. Scott County State Park is located twelve miles north of Scott City. It is one of the many attractive parks and recreational areas that have been developed by the state.

A Rodeo at Phillipsburg. For thousands of persons the high spot on the Kansas entertainment calendar each year is the rodeo. Bucking wildly, a Brahma bull attempts to dislodge a cowboy in the Phillipsburg Rodeo.

Cimarron Crossing, the short cut for the trail. Dodge City became known as the "Queen of the Cow Towns." Because of present day television programs, Front Street, the Long Branch, and Boot Hill are known in all parts of the nation. One of the principal streets of the city is now named Gunsmoke Street. Near Dodge City is a museum that has a good collection of Indian and pioneer relics.

Many towns and cities have places of special interest. Near Hays stands the old Fort Hays blockhouse that protected the whites against Indian attacks in 1860. At Colby is a typical sod house, home of the early pioneers. A large Indian burial ground has been found near Salina. The Old Oak that was used for a post office on the Santa Fe Trail still stands in Council Grove.

Near Hanover is the only station on the Pony Express route that remains unchanged. At Greensburg is a hand-dug well that is 109 feet deep and 32 feet wide. Steps lead down to the water level. Numerous other cities and towns also have places of interest.

For those who like to drive and visit the out-of-doors, Kansas has many interesting natural formations. Near Lindsborg one can stand on Coronado Heights and have a good view of the valley of the Smoky Hill River. It is probable that these heights were visited by Coronado. Rock City, located near Minneapolis, has in it over 200 large eroded sandstone formations. A natural bridge is located about six miles south of Sun City. In the southwestern part of Gove County are many large chalk rocks of various shapes

134

Kansas Industrial Development Commission

Rock City, Southwest of Minneapolis. Rock City is located about two miles southwest of Minneapolis. It is a group of about 200 large sandstone rocks and is one of the attractions of the Smoky Hills Region.

known as Monument Rocks. The Old Maid's Pool, a lake that was formed when an underground cave collapsed, is near Sharon Springs. In the Red Hills Region are many buttes and mesas, that were formed because of their hard caprock of gypsum. Many other such natural features can be found in each region of the state.

Hunting and Fishing

Hunting and fishing have been

Forestry, Fish and Game Commission of Kansas

Crawford County State Lake Number 2. Recreational areas have been developed in many parts of the state by the building of dams and the forming of lakes. One of the most popular of these is Crawford County State Lake Number 2.

Guy Von Schrilz

Fishing in Crawford County State Lake Number 2. This young lady has been successful in catching a good string of crappies in Crawford County State Lake Number 2.

carried on extensively in Kansas from the time of settlement. The presence of great numbers of animals, both large and small, when the state was new indicates that Kansas was naturally a favorable home for wild animals. The pioneers reported great numbers of elk, buffalo, antelope, and passenger pigeons. The plowing of the grasslands, the cutting of trees, and the increase in population have left less space for the large animals, but conditions have been improved for various small animals and birds. With much of the agricultural land in pasturage, hay, and grain crops, both feed and cover are plentiful. Water is available almost everywhere. The rapid increase in a number of animals, since the state has begun a conservation program, is proof that

Kansas still has great hunting opportunities.

Hunting is widely practiced in Kansas at present. Quail, pheasants, rabbits, and squirrels are most extensively hunted by day. Night hunting is especially concerned with foxes, raccoon, opossum, and skunks. In all, about twenty-four species of animals are hunted. Rabbits are the most numerous of the game animals and are hunted extensively. However, quail hunting by day and fox hunting by night are chief attractions to sportsmen. Some of the less frequently hunted animals include wolves, coyotes, civet cats, and muskrats. Ducks and geese provide considerable hunting about the larger streams and lakes. Cheyenne Bottoms is especially noted as a place for hunting water fowls.

Fishing in Kansas has had a history similar to that of hunting. In early times fish were accepted as a source of food. As people became more numerous, and various developments destroyed many of the fishing areas, less and less dependence could be placed upon fishing as a source of livelihood. This trend has continued, as in hunting, until the chief interest in fishing is recreational sportsmanship. Only a very small part of the fishing in Kansas at present is carried on as an occupation.

Two sets of forces, one of destruction the other of promotion, have been at work on the fisheries of Kansas. Destruction of fish has come about both from the fisherman's catch and from making the streams unfit for fish because the sediments wash in from the cultivated lands and from pollution of

the waters by city sewage and industrial developments. The pollution of
streams has been harmful, especially to
what is commonly called the game fish.
These include various kinds of bass,
trout, pike, and walleye. On the other
hand much has been done to promote
the fisheries. This has been brought
about through the expansion of waters
for fish, the production of fish in hatcheries, and the regulation of fishing
practices.

The fisheries of Kansas rank well
with those of an average inland state.
The state has about 4,200 miles of permanent, flowing streams. The larger
lakes, with some 308 miles of shoreline,
afford opportunity for fishing. The
numerous smaller lakes and the many
multi-purpose farm ponds likewise extend fishing opportunities.

STUDENT ACTIVITIES

1. How many of the state parks of Kan-
    sas have you visited? Which did you
    enjoy the most? Why?

2. Why is recreation important to people?

3. In what ways can people help make the
    parks of Kansas more attractive?

4. On a large map of Kansas mark a tour
    you would like to take. Which part
    of the tour do you think would be most
    interesting? Why?

5. What are five noted events that are
    held in Kansas each year?

6. In which natural region are most of the
    state parks? Why?

7. Why is Cheyenne Bottoms an unusual-
    ly good place for hunting fowls?

8. Which cities in Kansas are considered
    as tourist centers? What is the chief
    attraction of each?

9. Which state park is nearest your home?
    Have you visited it? What are its prin-
    cipal recreational activities?

10. On an outline map of Kansas locate the
    state parks.

Chapter 14

CITIES AND TOWNS OF KANSAS

Some of the early settlements of Kansas were formed where roads or trails crossed or where rivers had to be forded. Some settlements were made at places where minerals such as coal, zinc, or petroleum were discovered. After the railroads came to Kansas, settlements formed where railroads crossed each other, or where the railroad crossed an important highway or trail. Most of the settlements grew slowly. A trading post was started. Later, other stores, a post office, churches, and schools were added. When the first store was started the settlement formed a hamlet. As it grew, it became a village, then a town. Some of the settlements have grown into cities and helped to form metropolitan areas.

The Federal Government classifies all places with populations of 2,500 or more as cities. According to the 1950 census there were seventy-one cities in Kansas. Using the population figures for the incorporated places of the state as reported by the county assessors in 1958 there are eighty-five cities. These cities of Kansas range in size from places like WaKeeney, Scott City, Council Grove, and Mulvane, that have between 2,500 and 3,000 people, to such large urban centers as Wichita with 250,000 people and Kansas City with a population of 132,000. A metropolitan area includes a central city of at least 50,000 people and its suburban areas that have a density of population of 150 or more persons per square mile. Kansas, in 1950, had three metropolitan areas. The metropolitan area shows the true importance of an urban area better than just the area within the political city limits. Large industries that require much space or those industries that produce explosive, inflammable, or smelly goods commonly locate outside the city limits. Each city has stores, schools, doctors, lawyers, government employees, insurance offices, shipping, manufacturing, recreation facilities, and other activities which employ thousands of persons.

From the study of geography we learn much about why some cities grow and others do not, and why cities vary so much in their activities. We might think of an urban place feeding on a certain area. If the area is too small or is poor in resources, there is little chance for the town to grow. If, on the other hand, the town or city has access to rich resources, such as important minerals, valuable forests, or good agricultural lands, it will probably thrive. Thus, by studying the town or city as a definite part of the area in which it is located, we can understand much about the physical site and the general relations to other things. We are also able to understand much about the origin and distribution of these places. And further, we can realize why cities and towns vary so much in the kinds of business carried on, the extent of growth or the lack of growth, even something of what may be expected of these places in years ahead.

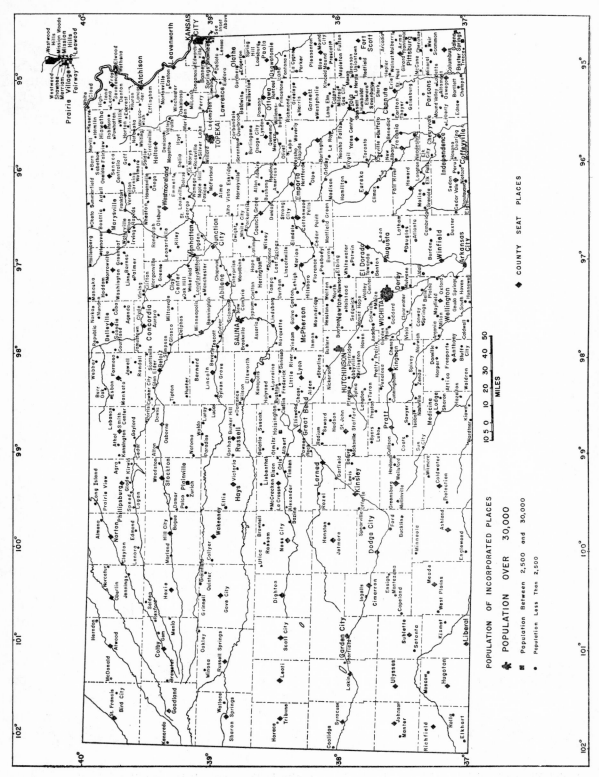

POPULATION OF INCORPORATED PLACES

🟌 POPULATION OVER 30,000

◼ Population Between 2,500 and 30,000

• Population Less Than 2,500

◆ COUNTY SEAT PLACES

10 5 0 10 20 30 40 50
MILES

Map 31. Kansas Towns and Cities

The services given by a village, town, or city are called its *functions*. Many hamlets and villages, such as Latimer, Bushong, Willowbrook, and Scottsville have only one chief function, the retailing of necessary food supplies to people living near. Such places as Wichita, Topeka, Kansas City, Hutchinson, Salina, and other cities retail not only foods but all kinds of goods, and people come from great distances to trade. The larger the town or city the greater the number of functions it will have. It will carry on transportation, wholesale, manufacturing, education, political, agricultural, mineral, and other functions. Great cities develop a kind of magnetism. Their functions are so numerous that people come to them from long distances for varied purposes. Regardless of their many activities, some cities become known for certain functions. Thus, some places, as Wichita and Kansas City, are known for manufacturing; others as Scott City, Kingman, and many county seats, are political centers. Still others, like Lawrence or Emporia, are educational or cultural centers.

Larger cities develop different kinds of areas within the cities. The retail district usually is near the center and can be reached easily by many streets and main transportation lines. This district becomes the busiest part of the city about which other sections are organized. Manufacturing and wholesaling tend to be established near transportation lines. The same is true for grain elevators and coalyards. Residences, on the other hand, tend to be located in the outer parts of the city where there are more space, less smoke, and fewer noisy streets. In the further study of cities and towns, various other things will be mentioned concerning the establishments of urban populations. Space is not sufficient for discussing all the cities and towns of Kansas; only a few will be treated individually, while others of considerable likeness will be referred to in groups.

Aerial View of Wichita. Wichita is the largest city in the state. It is a retail, wholesale, and manufacturing center.

Major Cities

Kansas has three cities large enough to be classified as metropolitan areas. Around each of these cities—Wichita, Kansas City, Topeka—several smaller settlements have formed, and the rural population near each has almost ceased to exist.

Wichita, the largest city in Kansas, was first settled about 1863 when the Wichita Indians established their camp on the site of the present city. Soon after the Indians came, a trading post was built and since that time Wichita has continued to grow. For a while it was an important cattle town on the Chisholm Trail. Being at the end of the railroad the city served as the shipping center for cattle driven in from the plains of Texas and Oklahoma. Although Wichita has gained in population each decade since it was founded, the city has had its most rapid growth since 1940.

The original site of the city was near the junction of the Little Arkansas and Arkansas rivers. From that location it has spread in all directions, but has expanded farthest to the east because of land better suited for the building of homes and factories. Many good city streets make it easy for a person to get from one part of the city to another in a very short time. The principal business district extends along Douglas Avenue and Market Street and, for several blocks, on the streets near this location. Many neighborhood shopping centers have also been developed.

Wichita is the leading industrial and distributing center for the state. The city is noted for its aviation industry, being one of the chief centers in the na-

tion for the assembly of airplanes. One of the largest planes used by the United States Air Force is assembled in the Boeing plant. In addition to the aviation industry, Wichita is important as a meat-packing center, for flour milling, for metal products, and for numerous other items. The city also serves as the collecting center for agricultural products. It ranks fifth in the nation in the capacity to store wheat and is one of the leading broomcorn markets in the United States.

Wichita is noted as a center of culture. Friends University and the University of Wichita are both nationally known universities. Many churches, some very large, have been built by different religious groups. Points of interest such as the Old Monger House, Riverside Park Zoo, Wichita Art Museum, and the Natural History Museum are visited by many hundreds of people each year.

Kansas City is the second largest city in the state, having a population of over 130,000. Located where the Kansas River flows into the Missouri River, the Kansas part of Kansas City forms only a part of the Kansas City metropolitan area. Near the city many towns and villages have developed. Three of these—Roeland Park, Prairie Village, Fairway—have populations of over 5,000 persons each.

Kansas City is an important food-processing center. Large meat-packing plants, flour mills, and dairies are located in or near the city. Many large wheat elevators are located either in the city or nearby making it one of the chief wheat-storage centers for the nation. Large stock pens, many with concrete floors, are located near the

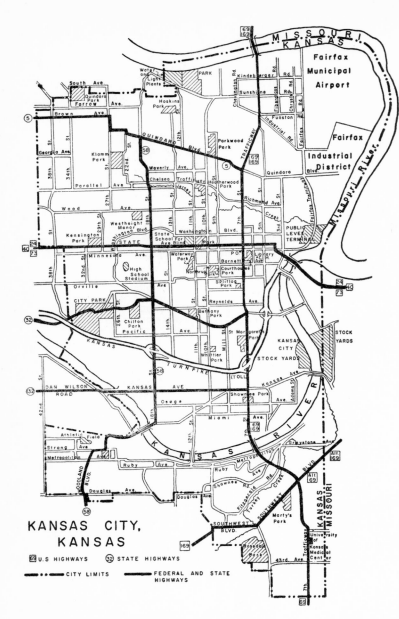

Map 32. A Map of Kansas City, Kansas

KANSAS CITY, KANSAS

🛡 U.S HIGHWAYS   ⬤ STATE HIGHWAYS

———·——· CITY LIMITS   ————— FEDERAL AND STATE HIGHWAYS

packing plants. The city is also recognized as a transportation center. Materials and produce can be brought in by barge on the Missouri River, by air, rail, or highway. The eastern end of the Kansas Turnpike is at the edge of the city.

Kansas City, Kansas, and Kansas City, Missouri, are connected by viaducts and bridges across the Kansas River. Although the two cities are in different states, in many ways they function as a single unit. People living in one city may work or shop in the other. The part of this metropolitan area in Kansas is expanding rapidly for many new homes and stores are being built, streets improved, and recreational areas developed.

Topeka, the capital of the state, is the third city in size. Although a few homes had been built in the vicinity of

TABLE 11

COLLEGES AND UNIVERSITIES OF KANSAS

SENIOR COLLEGES

NAME	LOCATION	YEAR ESTABLISHED	CONTROL
Baker University	Baldwin	1858	Methodist
Bethany College	Lindsborg	1881	Lutheran
Bethel College	North Newton	1887	Mennonite
College of Emporia	Emporia	1882	Presbyterian
Fort Hays State College	Hays	1901	State
Friends University	Wichita	1888	Society of Friends
Kansas State University of Agriculture and Applied Sciences	Manhattan	1863	State
Kansas State Teachers College	Emporia	1863	State
Kansas State College	Pittsburg	1903	State
Kansas Wesleyan University	Salina	1886	Methodist
McPherson College	McPherson	1887	Church of the Brethren
Marymount College	Salina	1922	Roman Catholic
Mount St. Scholastica College	Atchison	1863	Roman Catholic
Ottawa University	Ottawa	1865	Baptist
Sacred Heart College	Wichita	1933	Roman Catholic
St. Benedict College	Atchison	1859	Roman Catholic
St. Mary College	Xavier	1882	Roman Catholic
St. Mary of the Plains College	Dodge City	1952	Roman Catholic
Southwestern College	Winfield	1885	Methodist
Sterling College	Sterling	1887	Presbyterian
Tabor College	Hillsboro	1908	Mennonite
University of Kansas	Lawrence	1864	State
University of Wichita	Wichita	1892	Municipal
Washburn University	Topeka	1865	Municipal

JUNIOR COLLEGES

NAME	LOCATION	YEAR ESTABLISHED	CONTROL
Arkansas City Junior College	Arkansas City	1922	School District
Central College	McPherson	1914	Free Methodist
Chanute Junior College	Chanute	1935	School District
Coffeyville College	Coffeyville	1923	Municipal
Dodge City College	Dodge City	1935	School District
Donnelly College	Kansas City	1949	Roman Catholic
El Dorado Junior College	El Dorado	1927	School District
Fort Scott Junior College	Fort Scott	1919	Municipal
Garden City Junior College	Garden City	1919	Municipal
Hesston College	Hesston	1909	Mennonite
Highland Junior College	Highland	1937	School District
Hutchinson Junior College	Hutchinson	1928	Municipal
Independence Community College	Independence	1925	Municipal
Iola Junior College	Iola	1923	Municipal
Kansas City Junior College	Kansas City	1923	Municipal
Miltonvale Wesleyan College	Miltonvale	1909	Methodist
Parsons Junior College	Parsons	1923	Municipal
Pratt Junior College	Pratt	1938	Municipal
St. John's College	Winfield	1893	Lutheran

Topeka before 1850, the city had its real beginning in 1854 when the community was organized. A few years later it was incorporated and, in 1861, when Kansas was admitted as a state to the United States, Topeka was selected as the seat of government.

Transportation has always been an important factor in the life of the community. Near Topeka is the place

143

Aerial View of Topeka. Topeka, the state capital, is one of the most beautiful cities in the state. The capitol is surrounded by other state offices and business buildings.

where the trail leading westward from Kansas City separated to form the Oregon and Santa Fe trails. Later the Atchison, Topeka, and Santa Fe Railroad developed from here and still has headquarters in the city. Many state and federal highways lead to the city and the Kansas Turnpike passes just to the southeast of it. Topeka is easily reached from all directions.

The functions of Topeka are diversified. The political function is extremely important since it is not only the state capital but also the county seat of Shawnee County. Industries in the city are varied, including such activities as food processing, meat-packing, and making rubber products,

cellophane, mattresses, and railway transportation equipment. Some of these factories are unusually large. Many retail and wholesale stores located in the city serve the surrounding rural area and ship goods to other cities and towns in the state. Topeka has many fine residential areas.

There are many places of interest in the city and wide streets make it easy for these places to be visited. The capitol, located near the center of the city, is noted for the beauty of the building and its setting. Numerous parks and monuments, among them the Pioneer Mother Statue, Lake Shawnee Park, Gage Park and the Rose Gardens, the Museum of the Kansas Historical

144

Society, and the statue of Abraham Lincoln, are seen by many tourists each year.

Cities of 15,000 to 50,000

According to the 1958 population reports made by the county assessors, Kansas has eleven cities with populations ranging between 15,000 and 50,000. These cities have many of the same functions as those of the major cities. All have important industries, and together make significant contributions to the economic life of the state. These cities are largely independent units. That is, they have their separate areas for which they provide markets and in return do retailing and other services for their respective communities. With the exception of Great Bend, all the cities in this group are located in the eastern half of the state.

Coffeyville is the industrial center of southeast Kansas. Established in 1869 when James Coffey built a trading post near the crossing of Fifteenth and Walnut Streets, the city has grown slowly but steadily. When railroads were first extended into the area, Coffeyville became a cattle town. Later oil was discovered and the city became important for the production and refining of petroleum. Today, numerous manufacturing places operate in Coffeyville. Among them are foundries, smelters, pottery works, and brick plants. Since there are many good farms nearby, the city is also a processor of agricultural products that include grains, dairy products, livestock, and seeds. Coffeyville has a well-developed educational system that includes both a junior college and a trade school.

Emporia is a city of many activities.

Founded in 1857, it has become one of the best known cities of Kansas. William Allen White, editor of the *Emporia Gazette*, became known throughout the nation, thus calling attention to Emporia. The city has a wide main street with many modern shops. The residential area is famous for its beautiful yards, good homes, and clean streets. The principal trading center for a large farm and ranching area, Emporia is also an important industrial center, having about fifty factories of various kinds. Two well-known colleges—Kansas State Teachers College and the College of Emporia—are located here. The city is a transportation center. State Highways No. 57 and No. 99 cross United States Highway No. 50 near the center of the business district and the Kansas Turnpike passes to the west and north of the city. Emporia is a division point on the Santa Fe lines.

Great Bend, the county seat of Barton County, is a wheat and oil center. Located at the northern point of the great bend in the Arkansas River, the city is served by a network of good highways and the main line of the Santa Fe Railroad. Within Barton County there are over 563,000 acres of farm land. Approximately 75 per cent of the acreage is in crops, mostly wheat. It is not unusual for more than five million bushels of wheat to be marketed from the county during the year. The county is also a leader in oil production. In recent years it has produced over eighteen million barrels per year. These products make Great Bend a prosperous city. A refinery, large elevators, and numerous retail and wholesale stores employ many people.

Kansas Industrial Development Commission

Part of a Scene in Hutchinson. Huge grain elevators dominate this portion of the sky line at Hutchinson which is an important manufacturing city.

Hutchinson is the fourth largest city in Kansas, having a population of over 37,000 persons in 1958. Located where the 38th parallel and the 98th meridian cross, it is on the banks of the Arkansas River. The city is in an area of flat land. Its streets are wide and along them grow many maple and elm trees. Twelve large grain elevators that hold over forty million bushels of grain are located beside the railroad tracks. Under the city are large saltbeds. The city is one of the leading salt-producing centers of the nation and three major salt companies have plants there. Many large retail stores serve the people of the surrounding countryside. Retail sales total over sixty-five million dollars per year. Approximately 16,000 persons are employed by the various activities. Hutchinson is the home of the Kansas State Fair.

Junction City was incorporated in 1859 and is located where Smoky Hill and Republican rivers come together.

A wide main street, a very beautiful city park in the business district, and many good stores cause the city to be a successful business center. Nearby is Fort Riley, a permanent military reservation. Many of the people employed or stationed there live and trade in Junction City. Industries such as sawing limestone for commercial building, chick hatcheries, railroad shops, and making concrete products have been developed. Near the city is Rock Springs Ranch, the camp and training center for Kansas 4-H Club work.

Lawrence is the home of the University of Kansas, one of the great universities of the United States. Located on Mt. Oread, the University can be seen for long distances. Haskell Institute, a school for Indians, is also located in the city. Located on the higher ground and hills above the banks of the Kansas River, the city is almost midway between Kansas City and Topeka. Lawrence is served by the United States

146

Highways No. 40 and No. 59 as well as the Kansas Turnpike. The Santa Fe Railroad and a large airport also make the city easily reached. The principal functions are serving as retail distribution center for its area, an educational center for Kansas, and a residential center for the many students. Near the campus are large houses where many students live and several small businesses which serve students. Factories in the city process local food needs such as butter, ice cream, and flour as well as vegetables grown in the Kansas River valley.

Leavenworth is located along the rolling hills and bluffs overlooking the Missouri River approximately thirty miles upstream from Kansas City. The city is in a fertile farming area that produces much corn, wheat, and live-stock; thus, flour milling and meat-packing are important industries. The city is also an important furniture-making center. The expansion of Leavenworth has been largely west and south of the principal business district. Expansion to the east is blocked by the Missouri River and to the north by Fort Leavenworth. The Fort has long been a noted army center, having been established in 1827. In addition to the Fort several other institutions are located in or near the city. People working in each of these institutions live and trade in Leavenworth making the city an important retail center. Many of the older streets that lead from the business district are lined with large, tall trees and along them are many fine, old homes.

Manhattan, the county seat of Riley

Kansas State University

Anderson Hall on Kansas State University Campus. This building was constructed from native lime-stone.

Kansas State College

Kansas State College in Pittsburg. Pittsburg is not only the chief industrial and economic center of southeast Kansas, but it is also the educational center of this region.

County and the home of Kansas State University, is located in one of the most fertile areas of the state. The city has developed in a basin-like structure and low limestone hills almost completely surround it. The wide main street of the city, Poyntz Avenue, extends east and west. Along the eastern third of the street are many large retail stores. The university is located in the northwestern part of Manhattan. Buildings on the campus, as well as many business buildings, have been constructed of limestone quarried in the nearby hills. Local industries make use of the agricultural production of the area. Food-processing plants include a creamery, an ice cream factory, a cannery, and a meat-packing plant. Adjacent to the railroad tracks are large stock pens where animals are kept before being marketed.

Pittsburg, named for the steel center of the United States, is important as a coal-mining and industrial city. Near Pittsburg are large strip mines of high grade bituminous coal. The mining of coal is not as active an industry as in former years, but it is still extremely important. Many other minerals—limestone, lead, zinc, clay, shale —as well as natural gas are mined in the area. Included in the industries of the city are a brick plant, pottery factory, tile mill, and a chemical company that is located nearby. All make use of the natural resources of the area. One of the state colleges of Kansas is situated in the southern part of the city. Like most other cities in the eastern part of the state, the streets are broad and clean and have many large trees growing along them. Pittsburg is an important distributing center for southeastern Kansas.

Prairie Village differs somewhat from the other cities in this group. Located adjacent to Kansas City, it is a suburb of that city and serves largely as a residential center for people working in the larger city. Many of the people living in Prairie Village will do most of their shopping in Kansas City. A shopping center, schools, churches, and other activities, however, have been established. In general, the industrial development is of little importance.

Salina is the fifth largest city in Kansas and one of the state's leading industrial and agricultural centers. The city is often referred to as the "heart" of the hard wheat region. The elevators of Salina can be seen for many miles as the city is one of the chief wheat-storing centers of the nation. Four railroads and two United States highways make the city easily accessible. It is also served by one national airline. The Smoky Hill River flows through the eastern part of the city. Two large parks have been made in its meanders and a large golf course has been constructed beside it. The city has many factories, but most of them are small and employ fewer than twenty-five persons. Such industries as printing, bakeries, soft drinks, welding, and sheet metal works are to be found. Flour mills produce more than 12,000 sacks of flour per day. Since the city is the chief trading center for a vast agricultural area, the business district is large. Kansas Wesleyan University and Marymount College, two well-known institutions for higher education, are located in the city.

Cities of 5,000 to 15,000

In 1958 twenty-eight cities of Kansas had populations ranging between

Chamber of Commerce, Salina

An Aerial View of Salina. Salina is one of the larger cities of Kansas. It has a variety of industry and is the trade center for its area.

Entrance to Island Park in Winfield. Most cities in Kansas have one or more beautiful parks. This is the entrance to Island Park, one of the playgrounds of Winfield, Kansas.

5,000 and 15,000. The smallest of the group was Fairway with a population of 5,342 and the largest was Arkansas City with a population of 14,581. Most of the cities in this group are in the eastern third of the state.

Independence, Parsons, Chanute, Iola, Ottawa, and *Olathe* are located in the Osage Cuestas Region. With the exception of Parsons all are county seat cities and each serves as the retail center for its immediate vicinity. All have many well-developed manufacturing establishments, a greater number being located in Independence and Parsons than in the other cities. The processing of feeds, foods, and soft drinks is common to each. Also each city has printing and publishing establishments. Most of the factories employ fewer than twenty-five persons, but a few such as Portland cement factories employ more than 100 persons.

Fort Scott is the lone city in the group located in the Cherokee Plain Region. It is one of the older cities of Kansas having been founded as a military garrison in 1842. Today some of the old buildings still stand and plaques or markers show where others were located. Fort Scott is the trading center and county seat of Bourbon County. It has a variety of industries, most of which are small.

Atchison, Fairway, Leawood, and *Roeland Park* are located in the eastern part of the Glaciated Region. Fairway, Leawood, and Roeland Park are suburbs of Kansas City and as such serve largely as residential areas for it. Atchison, the principal city of a very productive area, has many food-processing plants as well as a variety of other industries. The city is important historically for its former river trade, as a starting place for many westward

150

bound wagon trains, and as the birth-place of the Atchison, Topeka and Santa Fe Railway.

Arkansas City, Winfield, Augusta, El Dorado, and *Abilene* were, at one time, important "cow" towns. Located in the Flint Hills, the livestock indus-try still plays a large part in the activ-ities of each. All are agricultural and service centers for the areas they serve. Each, however, has many things that make it different from the others. The chief industries in Arkansas City are meat-packing and milling. Winfield is the home of two colleges—Southwest-ern College and St. John's College. Augusta has a large petroleum refin-ery. El Dorado is a center for both oil activity and ranching. Abilene is a tourist center and famous for its early history.

Concordia, Russell, and *Hays* are lo-cated in the Smoky Hills Region. Each city functions around the agricultural activities of its county, for each is the retailing center and county seat of its county. Near Hays is located the re-mains of Fort Hays and within the city is the Fort Hays State College. Petroleum contributes to the activities in Russell for that city is near an ex-tensive oil field. Concordia is a small industrial center with about twenty-five factories in the city.

Larned, McPherson, Newton, and *Derby* are the cities having populations in the 5,000 to 15,000 group located in the Great Bend Prairie Region. Derby, formerly kown as El Paso, is near Wichita and is a suburb of that city. Larned, McPherson, and Newton are the county seats of their respective counties. Each has many good retail stores, wide streets, and beautiful resi-

dential areas. All are centers of agri-cultural activity. Newton is of special importance as a railway center as large Santa Fe shops are located in the city. All three cities have a variety of small industry.

Wellington is the largest city in the Wellington Plain Region. Noted as an agricultural center, the city is also im-portant as an oil production center. Like most Kansas cities, Wellington has wide streets, good residential areas, fine schools, and large churches. It is the most southern city on the Kansas Turnpike.

Pratt, Dodge City, Garden City, and *Liberal* are the four largest cities in the High Plains Region of Kansas. Each is the county seat of its county and each serves as the retail distribu-tion center for well-developed agricul-tural areas. Pratt is the headquarters for the Kansas Forestry, Fish and Game Commission. Dodge City is fa-mous as a tourist center because of its historic cowboy days, the Santa Fe Trail, and places of interest nearby. The modern city, however, is an impor-tant center of learning and industry. Garden City is the center of a large irrigated area. Liberal is located in the "heart" of the Hugoton Gas Field and is also a large wheat and broom-corn market. Each city is served by good highways and has adequate rail facilities.

Small Cities

Kansas has forty-four cities that range in population from 2,500 to 5,000 each. These cities are widely scattered over the state with one or more in each of thirty-one counties. In general in the small cities there are more small

Chamber of Commerce, Dodge City

Gunsmoke Street in Dodge City. This street is named after the famous television show, "Gunsmoke." It is an important shopping and entertaining area.

businesses. The market and retail activities reach restricted areas. However, these conditions vary among the different cities. Much depends upon the distance from the larger cities. Some places between 2,500 and 5,000 population serve rather large areas. Among this group twenty-five of the cities, like *Goodland, Anthony,* and *Eureka,* are county seats. This adds considerable business and importance to the cities.

Twenty of the cities in this group are in the eastern third of the state, fifteen in the central third, and nine in the High Plains. Some grouping is shown in the southeastern part of the state in the lead and zinc and the petroleum areas, and also near Wichita and Kansas City. The Glaciated Region has more than its share of cities of this population according to the size of the region. Many of these are near Kansas City and are suburbs of that city as well as Kansas City, Missouri. All of the cities are closely related to production within their respective trade territories.

Many of the larger cities of this group have something of importance in addition to the more local business. Thus, *Ulysses* profits from large carbon black plants in the area; *Phillipsburg* has one of the largest annual rodeos in the state and is near Kirwin Dam and Reservoir; in *Fredonia* is located one of the largest linseed and soybean mills in the United States; *Medicine Lodge* has a large wallboard plant that uses gypsum mined in the region.

As a whole the cities between 2,500 and 5,000 have shown little change in population for several decades. About 75 per cent of these places have shown gains in population, while 25 per cent have shown losses. Several of the cities with special advantages have made considerable gains. On the other extreme a few have had considerable losses. The newer centers are near large cities.

Towns and Villages

Towns and villages have much in common with cities. They perform many of the same functions as those performed by larger places. Each serves as a residence for many people. Each is a market for produce and a shopping center for its respective community. The chief difference between the town and the large city is that the functions of the town are fewer in number and smaller in scale. The town or village is related to its locality as is the large city to its region or to the entire state. A special function of the small centers is that of serving as links between rural people who produce foods and raw materials and city people who manufacture many things that the people of the towns and country use.

According to the 1958 report there were 526 incorporated towns and villages in Kansas. Of these, eighty-seven range in population between 1,000 and 2,500, and 439 have under 1,000 persons. Twenty of these places have fewer than 100 persons each. The towns and villages show considerable variation in distribution. In general these centers are most numerous in fertile agricultural sections, in mining areas, and about large cities.

The towns and villages reflect much concerning the activities of their respective communities. Many of the towns, such as *Hill City*, *Cottonwood*, and *Seneca*, are county seats. In most of these the courthouse occupies a plat near the center of town, with the main developments surrounding or near it. Most items marketed in the towns are produced in the local communities, and items sold are for local use.

The towns and villages have had difficulty in surviving. Not only have many people moved from rural areas to the cities, but, with good roads and means of travel and transportation, much marketing and shopping are done in the larger centers. Some of the towns have made considerable growth because of a new factory, a consolidated school, or some other special development. Most of these places have gained little in recent decades. About half the villages have lost population, and some have disappeared.

STUDENT ACTIVITIES

1. On a large map of Kansas locate the ten largest cities in the state.
2. Are the large cities of Kansas gaining or losing in population? List the reasons you think cause this gain or loss.
3. Which natural region has the largest number of cities? How does the natural region influence the size of cities?
4. What are the functions of a city or town? What functions does your community carry on?
5. What are the important activities carried on in each of the following?
   a. Wichita
   b. Garden City
   c. Pittsburg
   d. Topeka
   e. Phillipsburg
   f. Kansas City
   g. Newton
   h. Manhattan

6. What is the county seat of your county? How many county seats are there in Kansas?

7. In what city or cities would you find the following?
   a. State college or university
   b. Large meat-packing plants
   c. State Fair Grounds
   d. Large elevators
   e. Remains of historical importance

8. What are the three metropolitan areas of Kansas? What is a metropolitan area?

9. How many cities in Kansas have a population of more than 5,000? Make a map and locate these cities on it.

10. How do the functions of the cities in western Kansas differ from those in eastern Kansas? Why?

Chapter 15

THE FUTURE OF KANSAS

The growth of Kansas depends upon continuing the present program of conservation and use of resources. Streams once were polluted by raw sewage and chemicals which killed fish and made the water unsafe for use. Now factories and cities are turning to filtering plants to purify the water before returning it to the streams. Many of the impurities now are made useful as fertilizers and chemicals. Streams formerly were allowed to flood and destroy life and property. Now dams, reservoirs, and flood walls are being constructed to control floods and make the streams useful for power, irrigation, sports, and recreation. Although much has been done, much still remains to be done.

Formerly soil, the most vital resource of Kansas, was washed away from the fields and filled the stream channels, making them flood more easily. Now by extending grasses and pasture over areas that should not have been used for crops and by careful cultivation, the soils are being kept where they belong, and at the same time are being made far more productive.

Minerals once were wasted by poor mining practices and wasteful methods in using them. Modern inventions make it possible to recover a much larger amount of the minerals by better mining methods and by using the minerals in more and better ways.

Formerly the scenic areas of Kansas were not protected nor made available to the public. These scenic areas are now one of the most profitable resources of the state. A program of protection and development, plus the building of good highways and accommodations for everyone, is helping to make the state a tourist center.

In the past many communities were isolated and could not develop their school systems and health programs. Neither could they market their products or develop industries because of poor highways and poor communication. These handicaps are now rapidly being overcome by new highways and other communications.

Rural areas were once without power for lighting, refrigeration, and other necessities for attractive and successful rural life. Power lines now cover the state and every home can have modern conveniences.

Formerly Kansas had few factories to manufacture her many resources. At present there is a rapidly growing system of factories, especially small factories making clothing, processing food, and working in metal, stone, and clay. These factories are located in all parts of the state, but in greater numbers in the eastern half. The new factories are in addition to the meat-packing plants, flour mills, creameries, and other plants which were already here. Several new large factories, especially in the transportation fields, have been developed. All of these new factories are building a large, skilled, labor force and providing the background of services for the larger factories that are in the process of establishment.

News Chronicle Printing Company, Scott City

A Chapel Located at Camp Lakeside. The church is always an important part in the development of a community. This chapel is located at Camp Lakeside, one of two church camps located near Scott County State Park.

In order to keep these programs moving and growing, the state government has set up departments to plan and look after them. Also such organizations as local chambers of commerce and the Kansas Industrial Development Commission look ahead to see where help and promotion can best be given. Programs which these organizations have developed mean much to the future of the state.

However, all these programs for the betterment of Kansas depend upon schools and churches. The schools teach us the skills we need to have and to know in order to do the work required for all of these tasks. The schools also teach us to understand our way of doing things and how to co-operate. Our churches are the most important institutions, for from them we learn to understand the importance of the dignity of man, and the love of our fellowmen,

without which all of our programs would fail and our wealth would be worthless.

The people of Kansas must no longer think of Kansas as a rural state. Although agriculture and livestock activities are an important way of life, most of the people live in the cities or towns. The annual income from many activities exceeds the annual income from farms and ranches. All of this material progress, however, is not changing the love of the Kansas people for the country life and Kansas' hospitality to visitors. The future of Kansas will be more prosperous, but Kansas will still remain the state that her citizens and friends love and cherish.

The more that the citizens know about their state, the better they will be able to understand its problems. The geography of Kansas is an important part of this knowledge.

STUDENT ACTIVITIES

1. Make a list of ways in which you think you can help make Kansas a better state. Compare your list with that of your classmates.

2. Which part of Kansas do you like best? Why? Which city do you like best? Why?

3. What must be done to make Kansas a better state? What is now being done to improve the state?

4. Why must the future of Kansas depend upon a program of resource use and conservation?

5. What is your community doing to improve itself?

157

Appendix I—Counties of Kansas

COUNTY	AREA SQUARE MILES	POPULATION 1940	POPULATION 1950	POPULATION 1958*	COUNTY SEAT
Allen	505	19,874	18,187	17,025	Iola
Anderson	577	11,658	10,267	10,060	Garnett
Atchison	421	22,222	21,496	21,111	Atchison
Barber	1,146	9,073	8,521	8,651	Medicine Lodge
Barton	892	25,010	29,909	34,061	Great Bend
Bourbon	639	20,944	19,153	17,523	Fort Scott
Brown	578	17,395	14,651	14,540	Hiawatha
Butler	1,445	32,013	31,001	38,199	El Dorado
Chase	774	6,345	4,831	4,091	Cottonwood Falls
Chautauqua	647	9,233	7,376	6,316	Sedan
Cherokee	587	29,817	25,144	23,096	Columbus
Cheyenne	1,027	6,221	5,668	4,698	St. Francis
Clark	984	4,081	3,946	3,525	Ashland
Clay	658	13,281	11,697	11,008	Clay Center
Cloud	711	17,247	16,104	14,685	Concordia
Coffey	656	12,278	10,408	8,972	Burlington
Comanche	800	4,412	3,888	3,221	Coldwater
Cowley	1,136	38,139	36,905	37,113	Winfield
Crawford	598	44,191	40,231	40,352	Girard
Decatur	899	7,434	6,185	6,046	Oberlin
Dickinson	855	22,929	21,190	22,073	Abilene
Doniphan	391	12,936	10,499	10,678	Troy
Douglas	468	25,171	34,086	34,436	Lawrence
Edwards	614	6,377	5,936	5,567	Kinsley
Elk	647	8,180	6,679	5,369	Howard
Ellis	900	17,508	19,043	19,904	Hays
Ellsworth	718	9,855	8,465	8,257	Ellsworth
Finney	1,302	10,092	15,092	14,734	Garden City
Ford	1,083	17,254	19,670	19,804	Dodge City
Franklin	577	20,889	19,928	20,214	Ottawa
Geary	399	15,222	21,671	22,412	Junction City
Gove	1,070	4,793	4,447	4,158	Gove
Graham	891	6,071	5,020	5,222	Hill City
Grant	568	1,946	4,638	4,812	Ulysses
Gray	869	4,773	4,894	4,457	Cimarron
Greeley	783	1,638	2,010	1,916	Tribune
Greenwood	1,150	16,495	13,574	12,015	Eureka
Hamilton	992	2,645	3,696	3,019	Syracuse
Harper	801	12,068	10,263	9,922	Anthony
Harvey	540	21,712	21,698	25,073	Newton
Haskell	579	2,088	2,606	2,819	Sublette
Hodgeman	860	3,535	3,310	3,152	Jetmore
Jackson	656	13,382	11,098	10,455	Holton
Jefferson	549	12,718	11,084	11,394	Oskaloosa
Jewell	915	11,970	9,698	8,029	Mankato
Johnson	476	33,327	62,783	120,679	Olathe
Kearny	853	2,525	3,492	3,043	Lakin
Kingman	865	12,001	10,324	10,551	Kingman
Kiowa	720	5,112	4,743	4,702	Greensburg
Labette	654	30,352	29,285	27,180	Oswego
Lane	720	2,821	2,808	3,093	Dighton
Leavenworth	465	41,112	42,361	37,668	Leavenworth
Lincoln	726	8,338	6,643	5,972	Lincoln
Linn	607	11,969	10,053	8,736	Mound City
Logan	1,073	3,688	4,206	3,964	Russell Springs
Lyon	852	26,424	26,576	24,415	Emporia
Marion	959	18,951	16,307	15,736	Marion
Marshall	911	20,986	17,926	16,553	Marysville
McPherson	895	24,152	23,670	23,241	McPherson
Meade	976	5,522	5,710	5,329	Meade

Miami	592	19,489	19,698	18,457	Paola
Mitchell	716	11,339	10,320	8,921	Beloit
Montgomery	649	49,729	46,487	47,678	Independence
Morris	707	10,363	8,485	7,813	Council Grove
Morton	725	2,186	2,610	3,047	Richfield
Nemaha	709	16,761	14,341	13,519	Seneca
Neosho	587	22,210	20,348	19,678	Erie
Ness	1,081	6,864	6,322	5,692	Ness City
Norton	880	9,831	8,808	8,687	Norton
Osage	721	15,118	12,811	13,267	Lyndon
Osborne	898	9,835	8,558	7,638	Osborne
Ottawa	723	9,224	7,265	6,918	Minneapolis
Pawnee	749	10,300	11,041	9,458	Larned
Phillips	906	10,435	9,273	9,694	Phillipsburg
Pottawatomie	850	14,015	12,344	11,927	Westmoreland
Pratt	729	12,348	12,156	12,087	Pratt
Rawlins	1,078	6,618	5,728	5,102	Atwood
Reno	1,255	52,165	54,058	58,302	Hutchinson
Republic	719	13,124	11,478	10,248	Belleville
Rice	721	17,213	15,635	14,173	Lyons
Riley	624	20,617	33,405	29,685	Manhattan
Rooks	893	8,497	9,043	9,830	Stockton
Rush	724	8,285	7,231	6,469	La Crosse
Russell	897	13,464	13,406	12,581	Russell
Saline	720	29,535	13,406	43,238	Salina
Scott	723	3,773	4,921	5,136	Scott City
Sedgwick	999	143,311	222,290	326,961	Wichita
Seward	639	6,540	9,972	13,684	Liberal
Shawnee	545	91,247	105,418	127,470	Topeka
Sheridan	893	5,312	4,607	4,331	Hoxie
Sherman	1,055	6,421	7,373	6,234	Goodland
Smith	893	10,582	8,846	8,008	Smith Center
Stafford	794	10,487	8,816	8,078	St. John
Stanton	676	1,443	2,263	2,029	Johnson
Stevens	729	3,193	4,516	4,407	Hugoton
Sumner	1,183	26,163	23,646	26,892	Wellington
Thomas	1,070	6,425	7,572	7,003	WaKeeney
Trego	901	5,822	5,868	5,552	Colby
Wabaunsee	791	9,219	7,212	6,806	Alma
Wallace	911	2,216	2,508	2,286	Sharon Springs
Washington	891	15,921	12,977	11,644	Washington
Wichita	724	2,185	2,640	2,674	Leoti
Wilson	574	17,723	14,815	14,098	Fredonia
Woodson	504	8,014	6,711	5,750	Yates Center
Wyandotte	151	145,071	165,318	192,167	Kansas City

*1958 population figures are those reported by county assessors as of March 1; other figures were taken from official U. S. Census Reports.

Appendix II—Kansas Cities of 5,000 or More Persons

CITY	POPULATION					
	1910	1920	1930	1940	1950	1958*
Abilene	4,118	4,895	5,658	5,671	5,775	6,686
Arkansas City	7,508	11,253	13,946	12,752	12,903	14,486
Atchison	16,429	12,630	13,024	12,648	12,792	13,241
Augusta	1,235	4,219	4,033	3,821	4,483	6,183
Chanute	9,272	10,286	10,277	10,142	10,109	10,410
Coffeyville	12,687	13,452	16,198	17,355	17,113	18,121
Concordia	4,415	4,705	5,792	6,255	7,175	7,162
Derby	—	—	—	—	—	5,321
Dodge City	3,214	5,061	10,059	8,487	11,262	12,067
El Dorado	3,129	10,995	10,331	10,045	11,037	12,187
Emporia	9,058	11,273	14,067	13,188	15,669	15,166
Fairway	—	—	—	—	1,816	5,213
Fort Scott	10,463	10,693	10,763	10,557	10,335	9,983
Garden City	3,171	3,848	6,121	6,285	10,905	10,527
Great Bend	4,622	4,460	5,548	9,044	12,665	17,025
Hays	1,961	3,165	4,618	6,385	8,625	10,886
Hutchinson	16,364	23,298	27,085	30,013	33,575	37,492
Independence	10,480	11,920	12,782	11,565	11,335	11,497
Iola	9,032	8,513	7,160	7,244	7,094	6,921
Junction City	5,598	7,533	7,407	8,507	13,462	18,111
Kansas City	82,331	101,117	121,857	121,458	129,553	131,311
Larned	2,911	3,139	3,532	3,533	4,447	4,242
Lawrence	12,374	12,456	13,726	14,390	23,351	23,296
Leavenworth	19,363	16,912	17,466	19,220	20,579	22,638
Liberal	1,716	3,613	5,294	4,410	7,134	11,051
Manhattan	5,722	7,989	10,136	11,659	19,056	18,325
McPherson	3,546	4,595	6,147	7,194	8,689	9,083
Newton	7,862	9,781	11,034	11,048	11,590	14,170
Olathe	3,272	3,268	3,656	3,979	5,593	8,209
Ottawa	7,650	9,018	9,563	10,193	10,081	10,714
Parsons	12,463	16,028	14,903	14,294	14,750	14,191
Pittsburgh	14,755	18,052	18,145	17,571	19,341	19,450
Prairie Village	—	—	—	—	—	15,264
Pratt	3,302	5,183	6,322	6,591	7,523	8,054
Roeland Park	—	—	—	—	—	7,403
Russell	1,692	1,700	2,352	4,819	6,483	6,565
Salina	9,688	15,085	20,155	21,073	26,176	35,327
Topeka	43,684	50,022	64,120	67,833	78,791	101,155
Wellington	7,034	7,048	7,405	7,246	7,747	9,102
Wichita	52,450	72,217	111,110	114,966	168,279	244,671
Winfield	6,700	7,933	9,398	9,506	10,264	10,791

*1958 population figures are those reported by county assessors as of March 1; other figures, both population and area, were taken from official U. S. Census Reports.

Glossary

Aeolian soil. A soil carried by wind.

Air mass. A great section of the atmosphere that has much the same conditions throughout the mass.

Alloy. A mixture of metals.

Alluvial soils. Soils that are carried by water.

Anticline. An upfolding of rocks.

Aquifer. A permeable layer of rock holding water.

Area. A part of a state, county, or city.

Artesian well. A well in which the water rises about the water table from internal pressure.

Barometer. Instrument which records pressure of the atmosphere.

Barter. The trading of goods for goods.

Basin. The area drained by a river or a river system.

Border. A boundary or a line where a state, county, or area ends. A limit or edge.

Boundary. A fixed limit or separating line of a county or state.

Business district. The part of a city or town where the people go to carry on business. It is made up largely of such places as stores, offices, banks, etc.

Buttes. Small flat-topped hills with steep sides.

Capacity. Maximum ability to produce or hold.

Cement. Product made largely of limestone. Used in making concrete.

Channel. Deepest part of a river.

Chat. Refuse or worthless rock.

City. Community where people live and work closely together. Has population of 2,500 or more.

Climate. The different kinds of weather that a place has over a period of years.

Climatologists. People who do nothing but study climates.

Cloudburst. A sudden heavy rainstorm that usually comes in summer.

Combine. Machine that harvests a crop and threshes it at the same time.

Commodity. A product that is commonly bought and sold in the markets.

Community. Group of people living in any one place or area. May be just a few people as a very small village, or many people as in a very large city.

Condensation. Reducing to a denser form, such as water vapor to water.

Coniferous trees. Trees that produce cones, such as pine trees.

Conservation. Wise and efficient use of natural resources.

Contour line. A line that connects places and points having the same elevation.

Cossettes. Thin strips of sugar beets.

Cracking. A process in refining petroleum.

Creamery. Factory where cream is made into butter.

Crop acreage. Acres of land planted in a crop or crops.

Cuestas. Sloping plains, those with the upper end at the crest of a cliff.

Cultivate. To loosen the soil around growing plants.

Cultural surroundings. Educational, highly developed, and refined surroundings.

Cumulo-nimbus. A mountainous cloudy mass of condensed vapor discharging showers of rain, snow, or sleet.

Cyclone. A low pressure area. Usually a mass of warm or relatively warm air rotating counter-clockwise in the northern hemisphere.

Debris. Materials forced together as a result of some kind of destructive force.

Deciduous trees. Trees that shed their leaves during winter or dry season.

Degree. A 360th part of the circumference of a circle.

Density. Quantity per unit of area or volume.

Derrick. The framework or tower over a deep drill hole.

Detention reservoir. Reservoir that holds back or stores water.

Diversified farming. Farming in which more than one crop is produced.

Drainage. Carrying away of excess water by streams and rivers.

Dry-farming. Cultivation of land in a dry area in such a way as to conserve moisture.

Elevation. Height above sea level.

Environment. The surroundings in which one lives. These include both man-made and the nature-made things.

Erode. To wear away, especially to wear away the soil.

Erosion. The movement of soil by wind, water, glaciers, or any other thing.

Escarpment. A long high steep face of rock.

Evergreen. Tree which stays green all the year.

Factory. Place where things are made; usually has many machines.

Factory district. That part of the city in which many factories are located.

Field. An area of land used for the growing of crops or as a pasture.

Foliage. Leafy part of a plant.

Forage. Hay or leafy feed for animals.

Forest. Large area covered with trees.

Fractionating. Dividing crude oil into many parts.

Front. Zone of changeable weather between two air masses.

Functions. The services given by a village, town, or city.

Galena ore. Native lead sulfide, the chief ore of lead.

Galvanizing. Coating with zinc to protect it from rust.

Generate electricity. To change mechanical energy into electrical energy.

Geography. A study of the ways in which people are influenced by their surroundings and how they influence and change these same surroundings.

Geologic. Of or relating to geology.

Geologists. People who study the rocks and minerals of which the earth is composed.

Glacial soil. A soil that is formed by ice or a glacier.

Glaciated. Area that has been covered by glaciers some time in the past and had material either moved from it or has been covered over by material moved onto it.

Gradients. Slopes of the surface of the land.

Grassland. Land where grass is the principal type of vegetation.

Grazing. Feeding of livestock, especially cattle and sheep, on pasture land.

Ground water table. Top of the water level under the surface.

Growing season. Time between the last killing frost in the spring and the first killing frost in the fall.

Gully. Narrow, steep-sided valley caused by water erosion.

Gypsum. A white mineral used for making plaster of Paris and wallboard, and as a dressing for soils.

Habitat. Place where a plant or animal normally lives. Natural habitat is where plant or animal is supposed to have originated.

Humid. Containing much moisture.

Humidity. The amount of moisture in the air.

Humus. Decaying animal or vegetable matter that makes up part of the soil.

Igneous rock. Rock formed by the cooling of molten rock. Formed by heat beneath the surface of the earth. Lava and granite are examples of molten rock that has cooled.

Industrialization. The development of industries, generally factories, in a region.

Inorganic. That which is not derived from plant or animal life; metal.

Insulating material. Material which prevents the passage of heat or cold.

Irrigation. Watering of lands to supply crops with moisture.

Landform. The kind of land, whether high or low, whether level or rough. Principal landforms are plains, plateaus, hills, or mountains.

Latitude. Distance north or south of the Equator.

Leached. Washed out. Water, passing down through soil, leaches out minerals.

Legume. Plant that bears its seed in pods.

Lespedeza. A bush clover.

Loam. Earthen material that is a mixture of sand and clay particles.

Local relief. The roughness or smoothness of the land at any given place.

Loess. Wind blown soil; soil that has been deposited by the wind.

Longitude. Distance east or west of the Prime Meridian.

Manufacturing. Production of goods in factories; changing of raw materials into goods that can be used.

Map. Drawing to scale that shows where places are located on a part of the earth, or on the earth as a whole.

162

Mature. Fully grown; growth completed.

Maximum. Greatest extent; highest point.

Meander. The winding of a river.

Mesa. A large flat-topped hill.

Metallic minerals. Ores from which metals are produced; hard minerals that can be melted and molded to any given shape.

Metamorphic rock. Rock formed by heat and pressure changing another rock. Marble is formed by the action of heat and pressure upon limestone.

Metropolitan area. A city of at least 50,000 people and its suburban areas, having a density of population of 150 or more persons per square mile.

Mine. Place where minerals are taken from the ground.

Natural region. An area having many features of one particular kind.

Nonmetallic minerals. Minerals which are neither fuels nor metals.

Nutrients. Foodstuffs taken from the ground by plants.

Oil trap. Place under the surface where oil is stored.

Orchard. Many fruit trees growing close together.

Organic. Something derived from plant or animal life.

Organic substance. Something that has lived in the past.

Oxbow lakes. Formed when the meander of a river is cut off by the action of the river, usually crescent in shape.

Pasture. Large fields in which animals feed, may be either natural grass or some crop that has been planted.

Per capita. Per person.

Permeability. Ability of a substance to permit a liquid or air to pass through it.

Plain. Large area of level land, may be either highland or lowland.

Plateau. Area of level land, usually high, that has steep sides.

Porosity. Ability to hold water like a sponge.

Prairie. Area of level or gently rolling plain that is covered with grass.

Precipitation. Moisture from the atmosphere that is deposited on the earth's surface.

Processed. Prepared for market or further manufacturing.

Quality. Class, kind, or grade of an item.

Quantity. Amount of an item.

Quarry. Place where stone is cut from the earth.

Region. Part of the earth's surface where many of the things growing, or items produced by man, are much alike.

Relief features. Surface outlines of the earth such as valleys, mountains, and plains.

Reservoir. Lake formed by the building of a dam across a stream or stream bed.

Residual soil. A soil that remains where it is formed.

Sediment. Finely divided earthy material carried by flowing water, wind, or ice.

Sedimentary rocks. Rocks formed from materials deposited under water.

Shaft mining. Used to bring coal from the seams that are far underground.

Sheet erosion. The moving of the topsoil a little at a time.

Silica. Mineral matter usually occurring in crystalline form and used in making glass.

Silt. Fine clay-like particles deposited by water.

Soil. Mixture of earth materials and humus which cover the surface of the land.

Soil conservation. The proper care and use of the land.

Soil profile. A cross-section of earth showing kinds of soil in layers.

Solution. Dissolving of minerals in water so that they may be carried away in liquid state to be deposited elsewhere.

Sphalerite. A widely distributed ore of zinc, essentially of zinc sulfide.

Stationary front. A front where neither the cold air mass nor the warm air mass is moving.

Statistics. Accurate figures or facts regarding some subject.

Stream pollution. Putting things into a stream, river, or creek that makes the water unfit for use.

Strip mining. Where coal is mined near the surface.

Structural traps. Places in the rocks where oil collects.

Submergence. Sinking of the land.

Subsistence. That which is necessary to maintain life.

Technical. Specialized; exact in detail.

Teletype. Instrument used to transmit information.

Tenancy. Use or occupancy of land by paying rent in some way for its use.

Terminals. Ends of a route.

Textile. Material which is or may be woven.

Tipple. A building in which loaded cars are emptied by tipping.

Topographic map. A map which shows elevation by contour lines.

Topography. Variations in the shape of the surface of the earth; different landforms of the earth.

Tornado. Rapidly whirling mass of air that often forms a funnel-shaped cloud. A destructive storm.

Transportation. Moving of products from place to place by highway, railway, airplane, pipeline, highline, or other method.

Transported soil. A soil that has been moved to another place.

Tributaries. Rivers and creeks that flow into the principal river.

Truck farm. Farm that specializes in the production of vegetables.

Urban. Belonging to a city or town.

Velocity. Speed of movement.

Village. Small community; may be incorporated.

Water erosion. Movement of small or large particles of earthen materials by flowing water.

Watershed. A region or area that is drained by a river.

Weather. Condition of the atmosphere for a short period of time.

Wind erosion. The movement of small or large particles of earthen materials by wind.

The copy for the illustrations on the front and back covers of this book were provided by the Kansas Industrial Development Commission and used by their permission.

The illustration on the front cover is a typical wheat harvest scene.

A pioneer blacksmith shop is illustrated on the back cover. In 1827, Gabe Phillbert set up a blacksmith shop at Stonehouse Creek in Jefferson County. From this crude beginning has developed the great manufacturing industry of Modern Kansas.

INDEX

165

167